Funny Peculiar

Gershon Legman and the Psychopathology of Humor

Funny Peculiar

Gershon Legman and the Psychopathology of Humor

MIKITA BROTTMAN

THE ANALYTIC PRESS

2004   Hillsdale, NJ   London

Published by
The Analytic Press, Inc., Publishers
Editorial Offices:
101 West Street
Hillsdale, NJ 07642

www.analyticpress.com

Designed and typeset by Compudesign, Charlottesville, VA.

Library of Congress Cataloging-in-Publication Data

Brottman, Mikita, 1966-
    Funny peculiar : Gershon Legman and the psychopathology of humor / Mikita Brottman
    p. cm.
    Includes bibliographical references and index.
    ISBN 0-88163-404-2

    1. Legman, G. (Gershon), 1917-1999. Rationale of the dirty joke. 2. Wit and humor—History and criticism. 3. Sex—Humor—History and criticism. I. Title.

PN6149.S37L434 2003
809.7'93538—dc22

                  2003063859

Printed in the United States of America

10 9 8 7 6 5 4 3 2 1

"The watchdog's voice that bay'd the whisp'ring wind,
And the loud laugh that spoke the vacant mind."

Oliver Goldsmith, *The Deserted Village*

Contents

Acknowledgments

First of all, I need to thank Paul Stepansky at the Analytic Press for bravely taking on such an eccentric project, and Lenni Kobrin for her masterful editing. I also owe much gratitude to Judith Legman, for her hospitality in the home she and Gershon shared for many years in the south of France and whose attention to my manuscript has been invaluable. I would also like to thank her for granting permission to reproduce a number of extracts from her husband's frank and eloquent letters.

In addition, I am grateful to all at the Kinsey Institute for Research in Sex, Gender, and Reproduction in Bloomington, Indiana, for permission to reproduce archival materials; special thanks are due to the current Director, John Bancroft, and former Director Paul Gebhard, as well as Liana Zhou and Shawn Wilson in the library. Thanks also to Jakob Pastoetter at the Magnus Hirschfeld Archive for Sexology in Berlin, Germany.

Part of chapter one was first published as "Gershon Legman: Lord of the Lewd" (Brottman, 2001a). Thanks to Indiana University Press for copyright permission. Part of chapter three was first published as "Risus Sardonicus: Neurotic and Pathological Laughter" (Brottman, 2002). Thanks to Jennifer Mand at De Gruyter for copyright permission.

Archival materials have been reproduced courtesy of the Alfred Kinsey Collection, Kinsey Institute for Sex, Gender, and Reproduction; The Western Historical Manuscript Collection at the Thomas Jefferson Library, University of Missouri St. Louis; the Philip Kaplan Collection at the Morris

Library, Southern Illinois University at Carbondale; and the Nathaniel Tarn Collection at Stanford University. My thanks to all concerned.

An earlier version of chapter four was presented at the Columbia University Seminar for Cinema and Interdisciplinary Interpretation (Brottman, 2001b). Thanks to all my friends and colleagues at the seminar for their helpful comments, especially Krin Gabbard, Pamela Grace, Bill Luhr, Chris Sharrett, and Eric Monder, and special thanks to Harvey Greenberg for his response.

Also, for their interest and support, thanks are due to Victor Raskin, Martha Cornog, Timothy Perper, Reinhold Aman, Peter Rainer, and Mark Best. Thanks also to the students, faculty, and staff at Maryland Institute College of Art, especially Christopher Shipley, who has allowed me the space to conduct my research in a very special environment. Thanks also to my fellow clown-hater A. Loudermilk and to John Waggaman and Bruce Jackson for their photographs. Illustrations for this volume are the work of Ean McNamara (front cover art and pp. 64 and 106), Adam Hale (p. 82), Annie Gray Robrecht (p. 120), Melody Shickley (p. 140), and Dylan Andrex (p. 152).

Finally, to David Sterritt, for his unfailing support and indulgence, my love.

Introduction

Do you know anyone who has "a nervous laugh"? Perhaps you have one yourself. I first came across a person with a nervous laugh when I was 14 or 15, and I found it really quite frightening. My mother had been seeing a man named Andrew whom she'd met at the local pub. When I was about to be introduced to him for the first time, my mother mentioned to me that he had what is commonly referred to as a nervous laugh.

I think it was the first time I'd ever heard of anybody with "a nervous laugh," and the very thought of it scared me a little. Andrew, who taught geology at the local university, turned out to be a bald man with a very round, florid face, and his laugh was a terrible kind of wheezing guffaw that contorted his whole mouth into an awful flushing grimace. His laugh made him shake and sweat as though his entire head were about to explode.

And it happened *all the time*. That boisterous laugh of his burst through conversation like some kind of involuntary punctuation mark. Anything at all would set it off; it didn't have to be a joke—any conversational pleasantry, any unexpected pause. It would erupt even in the middle of serious discussions. But worst of all was that it seemed to make everybody else laugh as well—whether out of awkwardness, or because they'd also been infected by it, I wasn't sure. It even made me laugh sometimes, despite myself, partly as a simple nervous reaction and partly because there *was* something ridiculous about this laughter that was completely unwarranted, entirely out of proportion to the circumstances.

I found the whole experience rather creepy and tried to avoid Andrew as much as possible. Later on, after my mother had broken up with him, she told me that Andrew had a lot of problems and that he never wanted to do anything except go to the pub. She joked about how he smoked hand-rolled cigarettes and subscribed to a journal called *Soil Quarterly*. And he was always drunk. He used to drive the college bus, packed with students, blind drunk through the mountains. I also learned that he suffered from terrible depressions and would lapse into the most bleak and desperate moods. I had the feeling that this misery must have been very closely related to his "nervous laugh."

A couple of years ago, I learned that Andrew had died. He'd "drunk himself to death." It wasn't really a surprise to anybody. He used to spend every night in the pub, and often most of the day as well. He wasn't particularly old—in his early 50s, maybe—but he had a lot of trouble moving around and eventually started to become very weak. He lived only a couple of streets away from the pub, but regulars noticed that he had started turning up and leaving in a taxi. In the end, he couldn't walk, could hardly stand, couldn't really do anything except drink. And laugh.

Nervous and Other Laughter

Isn't it interesting how people can be defined and even transformed by their laughter? I've met people who laugh loud but not long, and others who laugh long but not loud. I know a man whose shoulders shrug up and down emphatically when he laughs, not so much as a side effect of his laughter but more as a sign, as if to say, "I'm laughing." And there's nothing more unnerving than witnessing a person you respect and admire laughing just as hard at the miserable witticisms of others as they do at your own smart repartee.

I once knew a girl who was much too heavy to be considered attractive, but I've rarely met anyone more popular. Everybody wanted to be around her, including plenty of love-struck admirers. She could have had her pick of men, despite her weight—and it was all because of the way she laughed. She laughed readily and with a wonderfully seductive, appealing sound, implying that never in her life had she heard anything quite so charming or so funny. When she laughed at something you said or did, it felt as though nobody had ever quite understood how smart and amusing you were until that moment; she made you feel as though nobody had ever quite "got" you until then. And that was the point—her laughter didn't transform her, it transformed *you*.

I also knew a girl who was quite the opposite. She was really quite gorgeous, smart, and funny—but it was all ruined by the way she laughed. She was a nervous person generally, smoking constantly and talking all the time, but her laugh made you want to turn immediately and run away. It was a loud, long, violent, and nasty sort of yelp, with no mirth about it. It spoiled her completely. Without her laugh she would have been good company, but once you had heard that horrible noise three or four times, it was all but impossible to be around her. What made matters worse was that she laughed at anything anyone said, whether it was meant to be funny or not, and usually topped off her laugh with a little tribute to the person who had set her off—"Nice one!" or, more often, "Good call!"

I once had a boyfriend who had an odd laugh; actually, an odd series of laughs, each with something different to say. He had a reputation for being great fun to be with, and I suspect that he went to some lengths to perpetuate this illusion. His "natural" laugh was a pleasant, lubricated giggle, perhaps a little more effeminate than he would have liked, which might be one of the reasons why he didn't let it out very often. More usual was a kind of loud barking noise, which I knew was at least half fake because it sounded so *dry*, as opposed to his real laugh, which was definitely *wet*. Sometimes, when he was drunk, this bark would grow loud, demonstrative, and just a little bit nasty. This happened mostly when he was laughing at his own jokes or anecdotes, especially in public. Once I distinctly heard him launch into a fake laugh that suddenly became genuine halfway through, when he unexpectedly "got" the joke.

Worst of all, however, was a laugh of his that resembled a kind of neighing bray, which sounded plausible at the beginning but always went on for slightly too long. When he started to laugh it was like watching someone take a seat on a Ferris wheel, but by the end of the laugh—when the wheel had turned and the seat came into view again—it was suddenly, shockingly, empty. Even if the laugh was genuine to start with, by the time it ended it had become a lie. And it was through the sound of those last, dry, false drawn-out chuckles that I was given my first glimpse of the anger and bitterness that constitute the nature of the constitutional pleasure lover.

Laughter in large groups of people always upsets and disturbs me, and I try to avoid being a member of an audience whenever possible. I especially try to avoid going to see "funny" movies. Unfortunately, however, it's hard to escape laughter at the cinema, whatever the style and tone of the film. I remember once going to see a series of experimental animated short films from Eastern Europe at the Institute of Contemporary Arts in London—a pretty safe bet, one might imagine, for anybody hoping to avoid outbursts of public hilarity. But I couldn't have been more wrong. So thrilled was the tiny audience by their cultural superiority, so attuned were they to the films' self-referential ironies and political critique, that they seemed compelled to express this intellectual acumen in the form of high-pitched squawks of delight.

That was the kind of laughter that loudly announces an understanding of the subtlest reference, the most arcane allusion, the most unorthodox pastiche. It's this kind of tittering laughter that ruins many film screenings, both public and private. In fact, film critics are sometimes the worst offenders in this regard, with their knowing snobbery lazily masked as tittering laughter, the kind of laughter that yells out, "Look at me!" At the 2003 Cannes Film Festival, for example, I attended a critics' screening of a self-indulgent but not especially ridiculous film selected in competition for the Palme d'Or. I witnessed the audience of "élite critics" lapse into the kinds of jeers, giggles, and hoots that would not be out of place among children watching a Christmas pantomime.

Even worse than film critics, however, are theater audiences. I stopped going to the theater some time ago for this very reason—because I find the kind of public laughter it provokes very disturbing. The last time I saw a play was four or five years ago, and even then I agreed to go only because I thought I'd be able to get out of it. A theater director had invited me to the opening of his latest production, an experimental play based on the story of three adulterous couples. When it turned out that I could not avoid going, I thought it wouldn't be too difficult to turn up, say hello, then slip off as soon as the lights went down. So when I arrived at the theater I was a more than a little dismayed to find that the director had reserved for me the seat next to his. Still, I thought he was sure to go backstage when the performance started, and it was with a mounting sense of horror that I began to realize that I was in a very makeshift kind of theater and there *was* no backstage.

Although the play was a serious one, it nevertheless elicited copious waves of laughter—not the thoughtless, blustery laughter of the movie-goer, but the whiney, goosey, tittering laughter of the self-styled cognoscenti. These awful sounds were provoked not only by the occasional gag, but by any reference to current affairs (especially politics), any mild piece of ribaldry, and—worst of all—any long pause, in which the play was not deficient. Unable to bear the silence, these patrons of the arts felt compelled to release their own mounting tension with irrepressible tweets and squeals of mirth (and among these laughters was the director on my right, who was just about the worst of the lot).

The final straw came when what was supposed to be a quiet and serious sex scene elicited a further round of squeaking titters, leaving everyone breathless with hilarity. I suspect these same tittering theater lovers would have a number of "issues" with this same scene were it to take place, for example, on an episode of *The Benny Hill Show*, where it would have been considered highly offensive to women. Such laughter, it struck me at the time, is the collective voice of a public paralyzed by fear, desperate for the externalization of any kind of comforting distance that will protect them from recognizing their own anxieties writ large before them in a manner uneasily, disturbingly real. Even more than a cinema audience, a theater audience is obsessed with sexuality, and afraid of it. I just couldn't stay there any longer, so I mumbled something about feeling queasy, got up, and left. The director later called me to see if I was all right. Although I did feel a bit uneasy about lying to him, I can still remember the enormous relief of getting out of that theater away from the horrible echoes of that trapped, tense laughter.

"Laugh and the World Laughs with You"

Is it just me, or are there more people with nervous laughs now than there were 10 or 15 years ago? Maybe it's just because I've been paying much more attention to it recently, but it seems as though there's nervous laughter all over the place today. Just turn on the television. Larry King a while ago had a show in which he interviewed the parents of murdered intern Chandra Levy, at the time missing for months and presumed dead. While Chandra's father broke down in tears three or four times during the interview, her mother grinned, smiled, and shook with nervous laughter as her husband wept.

The close relationship between jokes, laughter, and personal anxieties was made clear to me over and over again while I was researching this book, but never so vividly as during a course I took titled "Freud and Humor." This course was taught by a professor of psychology, a practicing psychoanalyst. It was part of an extracurricular program of extended study at Indiana University, where I was a visiting professor at the time. If I had researched this program a little more carefully, I'd soon have discovered that the people who enrolled in the course were mainly older people living in the retirement community where the course was being held. It was not a course of university-level study, as I had thought it would be. Rather, it was one of several classes that brought the residents together for an evening's entertainment—wine tasting, flower arranging, embroidery. Even realizing that this wasn't going to be the kind of academic class I had in mind, I decided to stick it out—and I'm very glad I did, because it taught me a great deal.

The class was composed of about 20 people. Most, apart from myself and one or two others, were married couples or widows. When the professor asked us to name our favorite comedians, the names that came up again and again were Jack Benny, Ernie Kovacs, George Burns, and Sid Caesar; the most recent shared point of reference seemed to be *I Love Lucy*.

I immediately disliked the professor. He was one of those confident, facile types who always win teaching awards and love to engage their students in the "dynamics of learning" by putting on what he, and probably most of the students, regarded as a highly entertaining performance. He carried a battered old leather briefcase bulging with important-looking papers, and his beard was carefully clipped to make him look like the Hollywood version of a psychoanalyst—possibly based on Montgomery

Clift in the movie *Freud*. There was a touch of the quiz-show host about his teaching style, which involved lots of animated gestures, plenty of anecdotes about his children, and endless clips from the Marx Brothers. He was, needless to say, enormously popular.

In one particular session, he went around the group and asked us all to tell him our favorite joke. Almost without exception, the jokes dealt with the anxieties associated with aging: fear of death, impotence, senility, deafness, colostomy bags, and so on, which vividly clarified, at least for me, the many connections between laughter, humor, and fear. One joke, I remember, told by a shaky gentleman in his 80s, was typical:

> Two old men are sitting on a park bench and complaining about their aches and pains. "If only my wife would die," lamented one to the other. "I'd get myself a sexy young girlfriend with long legs, blonde hair, a tight ass, and . . . (gestures with cupped hands in front of his chest). "I can understand the long legs, blonde hair, and tight ass," replied the other. "But why the hell would you want a girlfriend with *arthritis*?"

Interestingly, throughout his entire discussion of Freud's theory of jokes, the professor never once commented on the examples of neurotic and confessional joke telling that were being offered up in class every week and that seemed to provide concrete substantiation of Freud's theory. To me, however, the relationship between laughter, joking, and anxiety became increasingly obvious in the jokes told week after week by these stalwart old folks—and it was this, not the professor's lectures, that taught me all I needed to know about the psychodynamics of public laughter.

Incidentally, the professor himself told very few jokes of his own during this class, but one he did tell struck me at the time as rather significant:

> Two psychoanalysts are having a drink in a bar, and one of them says to the other, "Do you know, Dr. Schwartz, I myself made an interesting Freudian slip the other day. I intended to say to my wife, 'Could you please pass the salt, dear?' but what I actually said was, 'You've screwed up my life, you bitch!'"

Let us not speculate on the domestic circumstances that entered into that particular choice of joke.

Laughter in Theory and Practice

What is this strange thing we have learned to call "humor"? What does it mean for something to be "funny"? My intention in this book is to reconsider what we take for granted when we use these words.

To this end, I approach the subject of humor from a perspective different from that of most other scholars—I look at a number of alternative ways to conceptualize the meaning of this strange phenomenon. In the process, I hope to unveil some of the mistaken assumptions I believe dominate our social attitudes toward humor, at least in the West. Accordingly, this book is an attempt to defamiliarize not only the mechanisms and procedures of humor, but also its relation to the body and to the senses.

Fair warning: this exercise may lead you to a knowledge you might rather not possess.

First of all, it is essential to understand that, contrary to popular opinion, "humor" and "laughter" are two very different concerns, and they are not always connected. Physiologically, laughter consists of a mechanical or quasi-mechanical series of brief, uncontrollable paroxysms of the diaphragm and thorax, accompanied by short intakes of breath and a succession of vocal intonations ranging from a gentle gasp to a clamorous yelp. An efferent reaction of the autonomic nervous system, this bizarre series of motor spasms is often, though not always, accompanied by a twisting and contorting of the mouth and a baring of the teeth in a grim rictus, which in any other species would seem to signify aggression.[1] Indeed, as Joseph Addison (1712) pointed out, "If we may believe our logicians, man is distinguished from all other animals by the faculty of laughter."

---

[1] "We're the only animal that laughs. The only one," claims the stand-up comic Eddie Waters in Trevor Griffiths's 1976 play, *Comedians*. "You know when you see the chimpanzees on the PG Tips things snickering, do you know what that is? Fear. They're signaling their terror" (p. 62).

When considering the origins of human laughter, it is very important to distinguish between the biopsychological capacity to laugh and a characterological reliance on "social" laughing, with its obvious defensive implications. In their studies of the ontogenesis of smiling and laughter, psychologists L. Alan Sroufe and Everett Waters (1976) explain how an infant's earliest smiles occur in situations potent for eliciting positive affect and therefore appear to have an important adaptive significance. Sroufe and Waters examine how the infant's earliest endogenous smiles encourage bonding with the mother and how the sounds that make infants smile and laugh involve the fluctuating release of tension, which helps them learn the dynamics of arousal and excitation. Of course, this kind of smiling and laughter is spontaneous and innate and is very different from adult "social" laughter, with its psychological basis.

Most modern theories of adult human laughter relate it to health, vitality, happiness, and survival instincts. Humor scholar John Morreall (1982) proposes the universal formula that "laughter results from a pleasant psychological shift" (p. 39). Philosopher Dana Sutton (1994) argues that laughter is a "purgative," relieving the spectator of various "bad feelings" and encouraging an attitude of "disdain" toward its "targets," thereby generating "a kind of antitoxin that inhibits the target's capacity to induce bad feelings in the future" (p. 29). In modern psychology, laughter is generally regarded as a sign of mental well-being and a positive affirmation of the capacity for play.

The literature on laughter is enormous, although many of the important studies on the subject seem to have been to written prior to 1950, and most humor scholars disagree on a number of strategic points. It seems clear to me that this great volume of early writing attests less to our knowledge of human laughter than to the elusiveness of its meaning. Most of these early studies can be divided into three categories: the cognitive-perceptual, the social-behavioral, and the psychoanalytic.

More recent writers on the subject, however—such as Jenkins (1994), Sanders (1995), Peter and Dana (1998), and Wickberg (1998)—tend to insist that human laughter is "fundamentally" transgressive and liberating. Its transforming force is invariably regarded as having great therapeutic value; focused "humor therapy" has been applied as a curative treatment with apparently salutary physiological effects in the management of chronic pain, the encouragement of social cohesion, the reduction of stress, and the relief of suffering. Historical and cultural studies of the role of laughter tend to regard it as a creative affirmation of the spirit of comedy and carnival, an iconoclastic and demystifying sign of what 17th-century philosopher Thomas Hobbes described as "sudden glory," but without the connotation of crowing glee—pleasure in another's downfall—that Hobbes originally attached to this phrase.

Nevertheless, a few scholars and scientists have been brave enough to suggest that there is nothing funny about laughter and it is not necessarily connected to feelings of mirth. Biologist A. M. Ludovici (1933) suggested that there is something sinister about the process. He argued that "laughter is becoming no more than one of the many anodynes with which modern men are rocking themselves into a state of drowsy insensibility" (p. 115). Theories like this are clearly too disturbing to become popular, and Ludovici's book on laughter was never really taken seriously. Anybody who suggests, like Ludovici, that *all* adult laughter is hostile is invariably dismissed as a humorless misanthrope, even though such speculations go back to Ecclesiastes ("A fool lifteth up his voice with laughter, but a wise man doth scarce smile a little," xxi, 20). [2] As Ludovici (1938) pointed out, "Who could ever imagine Christ laughing?" (p. 115).

Morris Brody (1950) argues that the laugh is capable of affording only a partial release of tension. Unable to express the sadistic drive more directly, the man who laughs turns part of the sadism against himself.

Laughter . . . has a definite relationship to both masochistic and compulsive dynamisms. The depressed person, involved with his own hates, is unable to laugh because its meaning is too evident to him. The clinically recognized type of the fat, jolly person basically is an unhappy individual who denies his sorrow and in reaction-formation laughs at everything [p. 195].

---

[2] The same sentiment is echoed in a letter to his son written by Lord Chesterfield on October 19, 1774 in which he advises that "loud laughter is the mirth of the mob, who are only pleased with silly things; for true wit or good sense never excited a laugh since the creation of the world. A man of parts and fashion is therefore only seen to smile, but never heard to laugh."

Is it possible that human laughter is connected not to feelings of good will at all, but to a nexus of deep emotions revolving around fear, aggression, shame, anxiety, and neurosis? Is it possible that laughter is, in fact, the most serious thing we do in our lives?

In the process of studying the etiology of laughter and its relationship to humor, I have considered the work of those many philosophers who have been intrigued by the subject, from Plato and Aristotle to Hobbes, Voltaire, and Kant; from Schopenhauer and Bergson to Darwin, Freud, and Koestler. One man in particular, however, seems to me to have taken both laughter and humor more seriously than any other. This is the remarkable scholar Gershon Legman, whose erudition in the field is unsurpassed and whose investigation of this difficult and controversial subject is exceptional for its personal honesty and daring candor.

Once described by reviewer R. Z. Sheppard (1975) as "the Diderot of the dirty joke" (p. 96), Gershon Legman, who died in 1999, was completely self-exiled from the formal world of humor scholars, academics, and the cultural establishment in general. He had devoted much of his life to his two enormous scholarly studies of the dirty joke. But although his relationship with the academic world was always contentious, Legman was a genuinely erudite scholar who knew everything there is to know about comic erotica and who has an enormous amount to teach us about the way we think and talk about humor. Since his death, the importance of his work is becoming increasingly clear. In Janny Scott's (1999) obituary of Legman, he is described by Bruce Jackson, Professor of American Culture at State University of New York–Buffalo, as "the person, more than any other, who made research into erotic folklore and erotic verbal behavior academically respectable" (p. 29).

The bold subjects and quirky style of his work made Legman an easy target in the world of "serious" academic scholarship, but his writing quickly became widely sought-after outside the academy and finally developed a legendary underground reputation. Totally incapable of separating his strong personality from his academic writing, which rankles with deeply felt emotions and prejudices, Legman became most widely known and best respected in that demimonde of "outside scholars" on the fringes of the academy—a world haunted by ghost writers, booksellers, and those collectors of the obscure and arcane with whom Legman had always felt most comfortable.

And, in many ways, Legman provides a model of academic scholarship that seems peculiar and eccentric only because academics do not usually have much truck with sincerity. He refused to play by the rules of scholarly rhetoric. He always wrote in the first person, for example, and never used footnotes. He refused to pay any attention to the accepted boundaries of various disciplines and refused to separate his own private interests from his scholarly life. And, in fact, part of his ultimate goal was to demonstrate the arbitrariness of these scholarly rules and boundaries and to show the vain self-interest and pompous self-absorption of most scholarly institutions. In the end, Legman was exiled because he held up a mirror to the academic world and showed traditional scholars things they were totally unprepared to deal with.

If he were writing in any other field—literature, say, or art criticism—perhaps Legman would have been taken far more seriously, his passionate style excused—or maybe even encouraged—as a creative means of expressing some smart and radical ideas. Unfortunately for Legman, however, he felt personally compelled to explore the fields of sexuality (which academics have never been able to separate from the "objective science" of medicine) and folklore (whose methods also rely on rigidly empirical investigation). But Legman could not live and work within these boundaries. Like Freud, he remained convinced all his life that it was impossible to consider humor separately from sex. And by regularly giving us his own opinions of behavior and situations, and by consciously making value judgments about them, Legman shows that the "distance" and "objectivity" scholarly writers have established in these areas are no more than an artificial device to conceal the anxieties they face when writing about erotic subjects.

Gershon Legman was without a doubt the world's greatest scholar of humor, but he was also an authority on limericks, ballads, pornographic fiction, and many other forms of erotica. He was, in fact, one of the first modern prophets of sexual freedom. As early as the 1940s he was crusading to free print, image, and word of their hangovers from Victorian prudery. He was an enormously prolific writer; much of his work has been unfairly neglected, and a lot of it is now out of print. His take on the dirty joke and joke telling in general is basically Freudian in nature, and no one has taken Freud's writing on jokes and humor more seriously. Unlike many other post-Freudians, however, Legman was brazen and confident enough to extend Freud's analysis of the connections between sex and humor into many other areas of human life, and his conclusions about Western culture are perhaps even more wide ranging than Freud's.

No study of humor or laughter would be complete without reference to Legman's smart and funny scholarship. The truth is, however, that most scholars of comedy have been put off by Legman's antiacademic position, his caustic and witty style, and his often aggressive refusal to separate his own personal values from his philosophical theories. Even his enthusiasts tend to be squeamish about his tendency to launch into personal tirades, sometimes tainted by streaks of apparent misogyny and homophobia. As a result, this great genius of comedy has been virtually neglected by all serious students of the subject.

Let me make it clear that this is not intended to be a scholarly book on the subject of humor, but an admiring study of a remarkable author and a collection of essays on humor-related subjects, influenced both by Legman's style and by his ideas. The study of humor is an enormously evolved field, and humor research is fast gaining in prominence among academics in many different disciplines. Any humor scholar reading this book will no doubt discover that some of the most serious issues in humor research, such as the relationship between sex and humor, Freud's humor theory, and the connections between humor and laughter, are touched on very selectively and nonrepresentatively and mainly to fuel the momentum of my narrative. My regrets in advance if this is not the book you had in mind.

As well as an investigation into the psychopathology of humor, this study is also intended as an introduction to Legman's important and serious work on the subject. His work provides a kind of anchor grounding my own writing and connecting my various investigations of the many different things we in Western culture consider to be "funny." I also see Legman as a stylistic model in his refusal to ignore any example or illustration, however trivial or popular, in his reference to his own experiences and adventures, and in his ability to appreciate that, in dealing with such an enormous subject as humor, everything is connected. In fact, the real subject of Legman's work, as of my own study, is no less than the condition of being human, of having consciousness, and of living in a human body.

Legman's work is not only about humor and laughter, but also about those phenomena that historically inspire humor and laughter—comedy, jokes, clowns, and comedians. He was fascinated by the ambiguous, neurotic dynamics of public laughter, about which much has, of course, already been written, by Freud, among others. Legman, however, took Freud's ideas about humor one step further: he suggested that laughter, especially public laugher—the bodily abandonment to convulsions and paroxysms of anxiety—is, in essence, a kind of neurosis. Legman believed that most public laughter is not the laughter of relief, but a rictus of horror invoked by the symbolic, physical manifestation of the state of being human.

When anything ambiguous is described as "funny," people will sometimes ask whether you mean "funny ha-ha or funny peculiar?" a phrase most often attributed to author Ian Hay (John Hay Beith), since its first recorded use occurs in his 1838 play *The Housemaster*. Most modern dictionaries suggest that the word "funny" has a double meaning: the first being "comical, amusing, or entertaining" and the second being "strange, odd, or disturbing." It seems significant that the word has come to be split into these two, apparently separate, meanings—a process similar to that of repression, in which unconscious material is "forgotten," and obliterated from consciousness, at least temporarily. At one time, of course, the two meanings were simultaneous, but it soon became much more comfortable for the human mind to think of things being either just "comical" or merely "strange," when in fact the two meanings are essentially the same.

The truth is, it's all funny peculiar.

Funny Peculiar

Gershon Legman and the Psychopathology of Humor

CHAPTER *1*

Legitimizing Legman

George Alexander Legman was the only son of Emil and Julia Legman, a pair of working-class, Jewish-Hungarian immigrants who arrived in the United States just after the turn of the century and settled in the bleak industrial town of Scranton, Pennsylvania. The extended Legman family remained in Europe; most of them were killed during World War II. George was born on November 2, 1917, and it was his mother, Julia, who started calling him Gershon rather than George—a name he never used, except in the form of an anagram. Gershon was the only boy out of four children, and his parents originally hoped he would train as a rabbi. To their dismay, however, their son proved rather more interested in the flesh than in the spirit.

Legman claimed that one of his earliest childhood memories was making friends with a pair of eight-year-old nonidentical twins, Merry and Sherry, who lived for a while in the house next door. Since their mother went out to work, young Gershon and this precocious little pair had lots of opportunity for sexual experience, and this, claimed Legman in a letter to Christine Hoffmann, the daughter of a colleague, was his introduction to the world of erotic possibilities. "We invented—or thought we invented—both the '69' and the 'daisy-chain,'" he recalled, "and when, about five years later, I learned that we were *not* the inventors and that other people had figured it out too, I responded to this shock to my pride by determining to learn as much as I could about sex and sexual science" (Legman to Christine Hoffmann, February 9, 1976, Alfred Kinsey Collection).

Legman's father, a butcher by trade, was, claimed Legman, a stern and disapproving man, a "terrible prude." He was also, perhaps not coincidentally, a notable teller of dirty tales, whose lewd stories the young Gershon would often strive to top. To this end, Legman recalled, he began collecting samples of his fellow high school students' slang for sex acts and sex organs, as well as their jokes, swear words, songs, recitations, Johnny-told-the-teacher stories, and flytings or "dozens" (ritualized mock-insults that Legman—with the arrogance of a colonial explorer—claimed to have been "the first white person to encounter—among young Negro boys in New York early in World War II"). He also started clipping out the jokes from the *Literary Digest*, pasting them on both sides of pieces of paper, and then arranging them in files according to subject.

An older sister who collected examples in a small way first introduced Gershon to erotica in the form of a volume of Havelock Ellis, which their understanding, unshockable mother allowed to be stored with other forbidden books on the floor of her closet. Whenever he wanted to look at one of these volumes, claimed Legman, he first needed to crawl his way through a scented, ruffled forest of feminine underwear. One day, sitting among his mother's panties and leafing through his sister's volumes of Havelock Ellis, he was struck by a number of references to the work of a Dr. Friedrich Krauss. This was a familiar name. In fact, Krauss was the uncle of his mother, Julia Friedman, and had long been known to Gershon as his Great Uncle Fritz, well-established in Legman family lore as another remarkable storyteller, although Gershon and Krauss had never met. A prisoner in Nazi Germany during the 1930s, when Legman first came across his work, Krauss was the editor of two enormous series of erotic folklore published between 1880 and 1910—*Anthropophytéia* (*The Sexual Relations of Mankind*), and *Kryptádia* (*Secret Things*), a journal later edited by Freud.

At a very young age, Gershon was sent by his father to work as a breaker-boy in a Pennsylvania colliery. Unhappy with this job, and not particularly close to his family, he left home with his mother's blessing at the age of 16 and set out—as he put it—"on the road" as a "tramp kid" in the "cruel and dangerous world of semi-criminal men and sadistic cops" (Legman to Christine Hoffmann, February 9, 1976). In this dark and noxious underworld, Legman began his lifetime's work of field collecting, picking up every new or old example of lewd story, dirty joke, or sexual slang term he could find.

Despite a well-circulated anecdote about his being thrown out of the University of Pennsylvania during his first semester for stealing a type-writer, Legman never had the benefit of a college education. He spent a few months at the University of Michigan in Ann Arbor but quickly dropped out and made his way to New York, whose public library he often fondly referred to as "my only university." He recalled that the first books he requested to see upon arriving at 42nd Street were Friedrich Krauss's 44 volumes of *Anthropophytéia* and *Kryptádia*. He remembered being allowed to read those volumes for a brief time until the librarians discovered his age (he was still under 18) and took the offending books away from him. But Legman had already seen enough to confirm his sus-picion: Krauss and his contributors had collected examples of erotic humor and folklore from almost every culture and language in the world—*except* English. As a result, Legman decided that his whole life's work would be "to collect all the similar material in English, and to publish it, which I have been doing (on and off) from that day" (Legman to Christine Hoffmann, February 9, 1976).

In his early days in New York, Legman made his living from bits and pieces of hack writing: anonymous detective stories with titles like *The Poisoned Enema,* and *The Beaten Bride*, comedy scripts for radio, rewrites of theater plays, custom-written pornography, ghost written speeches and "autobiographies." He spent much of his time cowriting a series of erotic stories commissioned privately by an oil millionaire from Oklahoma, who apparently wanted follow-up sequels to his favorite novel, *An Oxford Thesis on Love* by Lupton Wilkinson, which was circulated in New York in mimeographed form in 1938. Allegedly, this mysterious gentleman needed a constant supply of sequels as material for masturbation, since each one satisfied him only once, upon first reading. The group of writers and illus-trators included, along with Legman, Gene Fowler, Anaïs Nin, Clara Tice, Clement Wood, Jack Hanley, Bernard Wolfe, and Robert Sewall. A num-ber of these sequels, known as the *Oxford Professor* novels, have since been published (Legman and Sewall, 1971a, b; Sewall, 1981).

Eventually, Legman found more stable work as a medical researcher ("amanuensis," as he descibed it) for Dr. Robert Latou Dickinson, head of the American College of Gynecology and the National Committee on Maternal Health, which later merged with the better known Planned Parenthood program. Dickinson was a retired gynecologist who had begun a second career as a sex researcher and had become the medical profession's most influential advocate of birth control. He led the crusade to persuade doctors to make birth control available to their patients and, owing to his medical specialty, had a special interest in women's issues. He was also a committed Christian who tried to combine the roles of doctor and marriage counselor. Convinced that a healthy sex life was the key to a happy marriage, he went about educating the public about sex and encouraging the attitude that sex was healthy and good for you. According to Legman, Dickinson was not only "cheap as cat meat" (Legman to Paul Gebhard, April 3, 1959, Alfred Kinsey Collection), but also a plagiarist, renowned for passing off other people's work as his own, including that of the sculptor Abram Belskie, whose birth-of-a-baby models, claimed Legman, Dickinson signed with his own name for many years.[1]

Each day, after finishing work with Dickinson, Legman spent his evenings in the New York Public Library, and left when the library closed at 10:00 P.M. He grabbed a sandwich and a piece of pie in one of the lunchrooms under the elevated train tracks on Sixth Avenue behind the

---

[1] Legman (1975) recalls a colleague of Dickinson's named Dr. Vladimir Fortunato, a "famous anatomical model-maker," who stole Legman's own invention of "a vibrating dildo of milk-rubber." "For my assistance in inspiring this invention," writes Legman, sardonically, "I was presented by Dr. Fortunato with the Medium size" (pp. 270–271). Legman (1968) referred to "an anatomical model-maker" whom he met in 1938, presumably Fortunato, who insisted he was the first man ever to have undergone a vasectomy. "This man, who was middle-aged, powerfully built, and handsome, made a pest of himself among the women secretaries at the New York Academy of Medicine by announcing to them, as several of them confided to me, the news of his vasectomy, coupled with the assurance that he therefore could not impregnate them, and seemed amazed that they did not therefore sink swooningly into his arms. The idea that birth control is all right in its way, but that there is nothing like *the spice of danger* never occurred to this modern primitive" (p. 796).

library. In his second volume on dirty jokes, *No Laughing Matter*, Legman (1975) reveals that on one such evening he was accosted by a stranger "with a Germanic British accent" who approached him in the middle of Bryant Park and offered him $5.00—quickly upped to $7.50 ("rather high for a prostitute of either sex, in the worst years of the Depression")— if Legman would go home with him for a night of "flatophilia" (fart-smelling). Legman declined the offer, but it was all grist for the sexologist's mill. Legman (1975) describes this incident when discussing the jokes people tell about such activities, which are, as he explains, "rationalizations, under the mask of humor, of a perverted reality that people who accidentally come in contact with would prefer to laugh about than have to take in all its ugly seriousness" (p. 885).

From 1935 until 1937, Legman lived in a small cellar in Brooklyn, in the home of bookseller Rubin Bresler, for whom he worked cataloguing books in exchange for rent; in 1937 he moved to more stable premises, at 50 West 76th Street in Manhattan. Legman's main personal interest at this time, and his first publication was *Oragenitalism*, a small volume of "Oral Techniques in Genital Excitation for Gentlemen" (Legman, 1940). His days of daisy-chains with Merry and Sherry were put to good use in this guide for men to performing oral sex on women, including advice about edible lubricants, stimulation techniques, the placement of pillows, and appropriate styles in masculine facial hair. "The beard and the mustache have in common a tendency to sop up the vaginal secretions and, if gray or white, be stained by them," claims Legman, advising that "the stain will not show in dark, nor—being amber in color—in blond hair" (p. 26).[2] He also claims that, after use of his manual, "the tongue in particular will have undergone training in rapid vibration . . . similar to the double-stops used in playing the flute" (p. 26).

The book's explicit depiction of oral-genital contact and its frank

---

[2] Legman (1968) makes the following point: "It should be noted that in spite of all statements to the contrary, oragenitalism is generally engaged in to give pleasure primarily to the oral partner and not to the genital partner; and when enacted simultaneously (the 'sixty-nine,' so called from the similarity of the position of the bodies to the figures 69) the usual complaint is that 'what is being done to one distracts one from what one is doing'" (p. 550).

approach to the importance of clitoral stimulation made it difficult for Legman to find a publisher; in 1940, cunnilingus was still considered abnormal and obscene, and this kind of discussion of sexual techniques would have been considered completely taboo, except perhaps in certain medical circles. Potential publishers who looked at the manuscript might also have been disturbed by the book's tone and style. Quite apart from the author's tendency to stray from his theme into minor bouts of polemic, *Oragenitalism* is unique in actually managing to talk elegantly about sex without being clinical, achieving the rare feat—rare in Western culture, anyway—of separating sex talk from medicine.

By 1939, Legman had managed to persuade the publishing firm of J. R. Brussel in New York to take on *Oragenitalism*, and the book came out in 1940. Jacob Brussel was a smart and energetic antiquarian book dealer well-known for publishing and selling erotica, including legally banned works, from his Ortelius Book Shop and other Fourth Avenue locations in New York City, as well as by mail order. Owing to the controversial nature of the book, Brussel encouraged Legman to use a pseudonym. Indeed, as Legman was soon to discover, in the world of erotica, no one was exactly who he seemed; authors seldom published from a traceable place, and the names and dates of presses and dates of publication were notoriously unreliable. In the end, *Oragenitalism* was finally published under the authorship of "Roger-Maxe de la Glannège," an anagram of "George Alexander Legman." Brussel and Legman put together a mail-order package offered for sale to doctors only; for $25, the discerning physician could purchase *Oragenitalism* plus a collection of unprintable Norman Douglas limericks and Henry Miller's *Tropic of Cancer*, which had been published in France but was still banned in the United States. It was quite a deal.

But it was a deal that never took off, since later in the same year, 1940, Jacob Brussel's bookshop was raided by the police; Brussel's printer's plates, stocks of books, pamphlets, and mailing lists were seized and destroyed, and Brussel himself was thrown in jail for the publication of various pieces of contraband erotica, including the underground "Medusa" edition of Henry Miller's *Tropic of Cancer*. Charged under the obscenity laws, he was convicted and sent to prison for three years, and nearly all the remaining unsold copies of the first edition of *Oragenitalism* were destroyed.[3] In such a moral climate, it was hardly surprising that Legman did not have the courage to undertake all the research needed for his second proposed volume on fellatio. Plus, as a heterosexual male, he lacked the detailed knowledge of various techniques in oral stimulation that made the first volume such a special book. But, with outside help from female and homosexual friends, a second, elegantly enlarged and revised edition was published in 1969 (when else?) and "is agreed to be the best book on orasexual techniques of all kinds" (Legman to Christine Hoffmann, February 9, 1976, Alfred Kinsey Collection)—at least, according to its author.

In 1942, Legman and his first wife, Beverley Keith, moved to 858 Hornaday Place, a tiny three-room cottage in the Bronx, a house that allegedly once belonged to the maverick philosopher Charles Fort. In the same year, to Legman's enormous excitement, he was contacted by Alfred Kinsey, then a Professor of Zoology at Indiana University in Bloomington. Kinsey, who had been writing to Robert Latou Dickinson for some time, had heard about Legman through Dickinson and thought Legman might be able to help out with Kinsey's book buying and general bibliographic research.

Alfred Kinsey had received sponsorship to do his groundbreaking midcentury sex study partly because he was a taxonomer of gall-wasps who was considered pretty much beyond moral reproach—a married man and former Eagle Scout. When he began teaching sex education at Indiana University, the position led him to be invited to undertake the largest sex research project ever—and he got the job because it was assumed, ironically, as it turned out, that he could not possibly be too controversial.

When he originally got in touch with Legman, Kinsey (1948) was working on the first volume of what was to become known, infamously, as the "Kinsey Report." In connection with this project, Kinsey was looking for someone to take on the job of ploughing through dusty annals of

---

[3] There may still be a very few copies of the first edition of *Oragenitalism* in existence; thanks to the police raid, this is now a very rare book, worth up to $7000. A copy was reportedly being advertised on the Internet in the early months of 2003.

erotica in the homes of booksellers and private collectors in New York. He needed somebody who really knew his dirty books, who could help locate such obscure rarities as the 12-volume Machen translation of the memoirs of Casanova, the English translation of Bloch's *Beiträge zur Aetiologie der Psychopathia Sexualis*, and the 16 original volumes of Richard Burton's *Arabian Nights* with their complex and lengthy footnotes on Levantine sexuality.

It seemed to be a match made in heaven. Legman was thrilled by this wonderful opportunity actually to make money from locating and buying dirty books; it was the perfect job for a person with Legman's eclectic interests in erotic anatomy and literary curiosities. And he also had the kind of access Kinsey was looking for—he was already well known among New York booksellers and publishers. Mainstays like Samuel Roth, Jacob Brussel, Benjamin Rebhuhn, and Esar Levine all helped provide him with rare volumes of "gallantiana" (also known as "curiosa" or "facetiae"): novels and literary classics with erotic themes, as well as more marginal elements of uncensored material dealing with sex and humor, like ballads, joke books, and the eight-page erotic comic strips better known as "Tijuana Bibles," many of which are currently archived in the Kinsey Institute for Sexual Research in Bloomington, Indiana.

Legman, however, was never an easy man to get along with, and by 1943 he had already managed seriously to exasperate his new employer. Kinsey first began to express annoyance with Legman over what comes to be referred to in the correspondence as the "penis article." Legman had apparently helped Kinsey to work out a statistical calculation for measuring the average length of the erect human penis. But Kinsey—a professional scientist—didn't agree with what he saw as Legman's amateurish calculations. To his credit, Legman seems to have been aware of the possible statistical errors in this study, since on August 7, 1943, he wrote to Kinsey: "Not having received any word from you about the penis article, I presume you don't like it. That's alright, as I don't like it a hell of a lot myself. Too sweeping a classification to make on a lousy 456 rounded-off measurements . . ." (Alfred Kinsey Collection).

Kinsey certainly didn't like it, and finally informed Legman that he was "no statistician." Legman admitted to having no scientific training, but tried to back up his side of the argument, at the same time confessing to another correspondent that he felt as though he'd been "found out" by Kinsey and exposed as an amateur. What made the whole situation worse, however, was the fact that Kinsey had started to suspect Legman of cheating him out of money. In May 1945, Legman was confronted with a very cold letter from Kinsey accusing him of deliberately falsifying bibliographic references for extra cash. After this falling out, Legman did very little official work for the Kinsey Institute, though he and Kinsey continued to write to each other formally and sporadically for the next 11 years. And despite his difficult relationship with Kinsey, Legman remained for the rest of his life proud of his early association with what was to become the Kinsey Institute for Sexual Research. As late as 1976, Legman was still referring to himself as Kinsey's "first official bibliographer" (Legman to Christine Hoffmann, February 9, 1976, Alfred Kinsey Collection).

In 1948, Kinsey published his groundbreaking study *Sexual Behavior in the Human Male*, the "Kinsey Report." In this volume, Kinsey published, to widespread controversy, the results of face-to-face interviews with thousands of American men who revealed sexual habits that were shocking and liberating at the same time. Most of the men with whom Kinsey spoke confessed that they masturbated on a regular basis, many described having sex outside of marriage, several had had homosexual experiences, and a few even confessed to intercourse with animals. In his analysis of these surprising results, Kinsey made a point of insisting that sexual activity should be separated from traditional moral judgments. He was one of the first to take this position in an official capacity, and his report, as a result, was the source of enormous contention.

Since Kinsey's assertion was one that Legman shared, it may have been that Legman experienced a certain amount of envy of Kinsey's sudden fame, especially since he had started out by helping on Kinsey's project and then been, as he saw it, unceremoniously booted off for no good reason. He did, however, get some revenge with the publication of a brief paper called "The Sexual Conduct of Men and Women: A Minority Report," attacking Kinsey's statistics as unbalanced and misleading. This report was written under the name of "Norman Lockridge," with a preface by "S. Klein, M.D." but was, of course, entirely the work of Legman (1948a). It did not really have much impact on anybody except Kinsey himself, who responded with a coldly furious letter that is partly reproduced in Wardell B. Pomeroy's (1972) *Dr. Kinsey and the Institute for Sex Research* (p. 74).

In an interview with John Vinocur (1975), Legman expressed nothing but contempt for Kinsey. He referred snidely to Kinsey's "faked and indefensible extrapolations of his sex-questionnaires of 5000 eastern U.S. white college-boys on the whole U.S. population and even that of the world" (p. 126). "There I was," wrote Legman later of his Kinsey years, "working for a guy that wanted to make the world safe for perversion. He was a horrible guy, who was really only interested in me getting him books on the flagellation of children" (p. 126). However nasty and unfair that sounds—after all, Legman had outwardly fawned over his prestigious employer—these allegations have recently been repeated in a pair of controversial biographies of Kinsey, by James Howard Jones (1997) and by Judith Riesman (1999).

The truth is, however, that the disparaging comments Legman made about Kinsey probably had little to do with Kinsey's alleged sexual experiments—after all, nobody championed sexual freedom more passionately than Legman—and more to do with Kinsey, with his background as a trained scientist, making Legman conscious of his own lack of formal education. Kinsey probably also made Legman feel a bit of an outsider in relation to the academic establishment represented by Kinsey and his group. "I have detected a subtle note of cool-ness in Dr. Kinsey's attitude towards me since he found out that I'm no statistician," wrote Legman uneasily to his friend Tom Painter. "He did not, however, offer any correction. Only reproof" (Legman to Tom Painter, March 10, 1944, Alfred Kinsey Collection).

Another reason for the break between Legman and Kinsey was the difference in their feelings about homosexuality. As his two recent biographers make clear, Kinsey was basically homosexual by inclination, with a strong sadomasochistic bent. Though he never said so at the time, Legman came to believe that Kinsey's work had grown out of his compulsion to "prove" that homosexuality is "normal." Legman claimed that "the measuring of penises was based on the same homoerotic interest" (Legman to Paul Gebhard, April 13, 1959, Alfred Kinsey Collection). Legman, on the other hand, maintained a strong aversion to homosexuality; he regarded it as retrograde and pathological. "I am not of the school that would have homosexuals jailed, castrated etc., just cured. And required *not* to propagandize for their perversion, and *not* to write attacks on women. (Who asked them?)." But, unlike modern right-wing critics of Kinsey like Judith Reisman, Legman was a radical with a conscious agenda to elevate heterosexual love over the male violence he believed was frequently a result of sexual bonding between men. According to his obituarist Paul Knobel (1999), Legman also openly confessed to having had a few homosexual experiences of his own, especially in his early life (p. 15).

In the spring of 1948, Legman and Jay Landesman, an antique dealer from St. Louis, began publication of *Neurotica*, a cheeky little lay Freudian quarterly that became popular in the late 40s and 50s. Featuring early work by Marshall McLuhan, Lawrence Durrell, Allen Ginsburg, Leonard Bernstein, Judith Malina, and others, *Neurotica* was a smart mixture of literature and psychoanalysis and is now remembered mainly as the journal of the Beat writers. Vaguely dedicated to the proposition that a great deal could be said about "a culture clearly going insane," it was often daring, and always interesting. Landesman set out the magazine's aims:

> *Neurotica* is a literary exposition, defense, and correlation of the problems and personalities that in our culture are defined as "neurotic." It is said that if you tie a piece of red cloth to a gull's leg its fellow-gulls will peck it to pieces: and *Neurotica* wishes to draw an analog to this observation and the plight of today's creative "anxious" man. We are interested in exploring the creativeness of this man who has been forced to live underground [Landesman and Legman, 1948].

The early issues contained articles that mixed a serious intellectual tone with outlandish and controversial subjects, such as a piece on prostitution as a force for social good and another on homosexuals who marry women. Another article covered fetishists like "Jack the Snipper," a local fiend who secretly cut off locks of women's hair in the cinema. Another analyzed the attractions and drawbacks of the bar as a pick-up place. In one issue a classified section turned up, complete with ads for sexual curiosa, the most notable a purported plea by a "strapping young woman" in search of a partner with sadomasochistic interests. The next issue carried 18 pages of replies, many of them pathetic, and the classified page bore the notice "the degenerates' corner has been discontinued." Sadly, the journal lasted for only nine issues before closing down after a legal battle over a piece on the castration complex (by Legman—who else?). *Neurotica* gave Legman his first national audience, a few thousand readers, some of whom still remember the magazine very fondly.

Since Landesman lived in St. Louis, he needed a New York representative for the magazine and, on a trip to the city, offered the post to writer John Clellan Holmes. A researcher for *Time* magazine named Louise Doherty had mentioned to Holmes that Gershon Legman's essays on censorship in popular culture—the beginnings of what was eventually to become his book *Love & Death* (1949)—were the most brilliant work she'd ever read, though completely unpublishable. So, before returning to St. Louis in July, Landesman and Holmes took a trip to visit Legman at his home in the Bronx, a visit that is chronicled at length in Holmes's (1967) memoir.

The 31-year-old Legman is described by Holmes as resembling "a small, belligerent facsimile of Balzac" with "an unkempt walrus moustache almost arrogantly obscuring curled lips, a leonine shock of hair disheveled on a huge head, with hot quick eyes that were at once inquisitive and repudiating, as if they had 'expected no better'" (p. 18). Legman had seen both early issues of *Neurotica*, and although dismissing them as "mostly garbage" (p. 18), still offered Landesman his early drafts of *Love & Death*—already rejected by over 30 publishers, Legman noted proudly—to consider for publication. His spiel, recalls Holmes, "was headlong, iconoclastic, funny, rash, irresistible. It was like listening to a Mencken version of a Lenny Bruce routine. You laughed through your wince" (p. 19). His essays, too, contained "pages of such power that they struck me, even through my weariness and all the stale cigarette smoke, as the most fiercely beautiful polemic that I had read since Marx on the working day" (p. 19).

Later, Holmes and Legman became close friends, and Legman started helping out with the editing of *Neurotica*; he gave advice about bindings, type fonts, and where to get cheap bond paper. His connection with the magazine began with issue No. 3, which contained an extract from *Love & Death* called "The Psychopathology of the Comics," and he eventually took over the editorship, contributing articles until he left New York in 1953. The entire run of the magazine was eventually reprinted as *The Compleat Neurotica.*

At the time, as throughout most of his life, in fact, Legman was living from hand to mouth, working as a cataloguer and journeyman carpenter for the booksellers along lower Fourth Avenue to put food on the table for himself and his wife, Beverley. His only expenses were rare books and offal from the butcher, with which they fed their huge brood of stray cats. Even at this early stage, he had an enormous collection of arcane erotica and rare lexicographies as well as a massive accumulation of correspondence, erotic photographs, and comic books meticulously filed in wooden cabinets. He worked compulsively; in the year Holmes remembers him, apart from writing *Love & Death*, Legman was also compiling a supplement to the *Oxford Dictionary* containing banned words; an enormous collection of erotic limericks; the first of a series of folklore studies, later published as *The Horn Book* (Legman, 1964a); and, with his wife, Beverley, a translation of Alfred Jarry's (1898) *Ubu Roi.*

Holmes (1967) describes the Legmans' cottage as quite impoverished—almost bare of furniture. The bed served as a couch by day, boxes made do as end tables, and everything looked as though it had recently been rescued from the dump. And yet there were books everywhere, he recalls, "books overflowing the shelves on every available wall, books stacked under the desk, cartons of books, books lining the window sills, books in the *back* of books" (p. 21). And these were not antiquated volumes of fiction or poetry but a real working library, Legman's arsenal of dictionaries, lexicons, thesauruses, indexes, and manuals on every imaginable aspect of humor and sexuality. "By the time I met Legman," writes Holmes, "The work and the life were indistinguishable," but "what fortuitous collision of circumstances and predilections had guided him to his destiny, I never learned to my own satisfaction" (p. 23).

Holmes admits that Legman could be quite nasty, especially to anyone who had a secret layer of apathy, compromise, or dishonesty—his intuitive faculty was apparently uncanny. But, Holmes claims, despite this unnerving directness, people always left Legman feeling better than they felt before—a process that Holmes and Landesman came to call "The Purification":

> It took me a long time to realize that people went away from Legman—their psyches stripped naked, their defenses in tatters, their nerves in that odd *hum* of exhaustion—feeling somehow incalculably better than they had felt when they came. For there was an aura of total freedom about him, of honesty without mercy, of having nothing to lose, that made you realize that your usual social armor was unnecessary, slightly silly, an impediment—even as he hacked away at it like some psychiatric Genghis Khan [Holmes, 1967, p. 27].

"Legman," recalls Landesman, "had a staggering effect on me. He utterly changed my life, and I was devoted to his way of thinking" (p. 32). Holmes's portrait of the young Legman is a picture of a brave man who was unable to restrain himself from telling the truth as he saw it and who was, in his absolute conviction in the power of human sexuality, the only real revolutionary around.

Predictably, however, Legman was offended by Holmes's memoir of him; he described it in a letter to publisher Nathaniel Tarn as "entirely a libelous attack against me, under the cover of a journalistic (and saleable) 'I-knew-him-when' approach" (Legman to Nathaniel Tarn, April 26, 1968, Nathaniel Tarn Papers). Legman (1975) referred to it as a "sentimental-*cum*-snide presumed biographical sketch of me," taking particular exception to Holmes's claim that he indulged in "fake-folklore" and "sexual gossip," which included "the attribution of homosexuality to famous artists and political figures on no evidence" (p. 426). He also objected to Holmes's claim that he was a "walking dossier of scandalous info about the sex habits of politicians, actors and Roman Catholic Cardinals" and that he once described Shakespeare in conversation as "hardly more than a talented fruit" (p. 426).

The year 1949 saw the publication, at long last, of what Legman would continue to refer to all through his life as his best book. *Love &*

Death had been accepted in 1948 by a New York publishing firm, New Directions, and announced as No. 8 in the "Directions" series. But when the firm's director, James Laughlin, finally read through the proofs, he came to realize that the book was utterly unprintable. Legman's hints about the sex lives of famous people and his ruthless disclosure of aliases and pseudonyms convinced Laughlin that the book would be libelous. When Legman refused to make the changes requested, his contract was canceled and the manuscript returned. The book was finally published the following year by Breaking Point—actually Legman himself, funded by his friend and fellow sexologist Osmond Beckwith. He used the type saved from the printing of *Neurotica*, except for a new title page and page headings designed and sometimes set up by the author, line by line and page by page. It was Legman's own whim, for example, to glorify the ampersand in the title: *Love & Death* never appears in any other form. He then used the back cover of *Neurotica* to promote the book; he listed 42 publishers that had apparently already rejected it.

A collection of four essays on the state of popular culture, *Love & Death* was printed in a run of only two thousand and sold mainly at the Eighth Street Bookshop in New York. The price was 1.00; profits had been discounted beforehand. It was out of print a few months after going on sale, and Legman could not afford to reprint. Nevertheless, *Love & Death* is perhaps Legman's most influential work because of its radical criticism of the substitution of violence for sex in literature, popular novels, and comics. French translations of the sections on violence in the comics (1948b) and on the "bitch-heroine" (1950a) appeared in *Les Temps Modernes*. In 1968, Legman was negotiating with publishers about a British edition of *Love & Death*, especially in the wake of the Brady/Hindley "Moors Murders." "It has taken you chaps in England twenty years to wake up to *Love & Death*," he wrote to Nathaniel Tarn at Cape Editions, "that, and perhaps the cannibalized bodies of a couple of helpless tykes out on the Moors . . . quite aside from Fiedler's helpful plagiaristic publicizing" (Legman to Nathaniel Tarn, April 26, 1968, Nathaniel Tarn Papers).[4]

---

[4] In fact, there was no cannibalism involved in the Brady/Hindley murders. Legman here accuses critic Leslie Fiedler of plagiarizing the title of his famous

Love & Death, which contains most of Legman's *Neurotica* essays, had considerable influence on many social and literary critics, including Leslie Fiedler, as Legman pointed out. The basic premise of the book is that the increasing sadism and violence of American culture is the direct result of society's relentless suppression of sex:

> Murder having replaced sex in the popular arts, the glorification of one requires the degradation of the other . . . so that we are faced in our culture by the insurmountable schizophrenic contradiction that sex, which is legal in fact, is a crime on paper, while murder—a crime in fact—is, on paper, the best-seller of all time. Can anyone explain this double-standard before it blows up the world? [Legman, 1949, p. 11].

The book is a brilliant, intemperate Jeremiad arguing that not sex but violence—including patriarchy's oppression of women—is the *real* pornography and explaining how our values are distorted when we glorify violence and criticize sex.

---

work *Love and Death in the American Novel.* Legman adds that "it is very possible that all my intended audience there among the young people of Britain may be conked out by then on precisely the sort of drugs that Prof. Fiedler is propagandizing *for*" (Legman to Nathaniel Tarn, April 26, 1968, Nathaniel Tarn Papers). In an earlier letter to Tarn, who suggested that Fiedler be approached to write the preface for the British edition of *Love & Death*, Legman writes "[Fiedler's] prominence is of course entirely based on his crude plagiarism of both my subject and style—a heady wine—in a work for which he impudently stole the identical title (not original with me, of course: it has first been used centuries ago in the 'Song of Songs' and elsewhere). When my book *Love & Death* first appeared, he wrote a gruelingly objectionable review of it, though obviously it affected him deeply, as he then sat down to rewrite it in 600 pages!" (Legman to Nathaniel Tarn, December 15, 1967, Nathaniel Tarn Papers). Other scholars Legman suggests might be better suited to write the preface include Alex Comfort (later well known as the author of *The Joy of Sex*), Jack Lindsay, Frederic Wertham, and George Steiner. A Cape edition of *Love & Death* never appeared, but a second edition was published by Hacker Art Books of New York in 1985, and Jonathan Cape published British editions of a number of Legman's other works, including *The Horn Book* and *Rationale of the Dirty Joke.*

To Legman, *Love & Death* was merely the opening salvo in his campaign to expose the sexual hypocrisies of contemporary American culture, his enormous, stubborn, exhaustive battle to bring some overall coherence to the emotional plight of industrialized man. The work was way ahead of its time, way ahead of the "media-effects" debate that is a commonplace today, way ahead of any discussions of the social influence of media violence. And, although Legman was more interested in the repression of sex than in the prevalence of violence, his criticism of the content of horror comics was taken up far more prominently by the much-abused Frederic Wertham (1954). Wertham was instrumental in drawing up the Magazine Association of America Comics Code in 1957, which prohibited "scenes of excessive violence . . . brutal torture, excessive and unnecessary knife and gun play, physical agony, gory and gruesome crimes" (p. 4).

Surprisingly enough, for a self-published book with a pretty small print-run, *Love & Death* actually seems to have had a significant impact on the multimillion dollar comics industry. By 1949, 180 new comic titles had been issued, all dealing with love rather than violence. The comic-book industry generally excused itself from the accusation that it promoted violence by claiming that such titles were issued "by popular demand." Legman (1950b) noted that the emphasis of popular comics seemed to have shifted from crime in 1948 to love in 1949—evidence, he suggested, of the powerful influence of *Love & Death*. Equally significantly, perhaps, the book was widely and sometimes flatteringly reviewed. Malcolm Cowley (1949) reported, a trifle acidly, that "Legman is the sort of critic who likes to ride his argument over fences and into the ground" (p. 18). The major holdout was *The New York Times Book Review*, and Legman's friend William Carlos Williams (1949) took care of the omission by including *Love & Death* in a roundup of the 10 best books he had read that year (p. 6BR).

Love & Death also contained the seeds of Legman's estrangement from the established world of large publishers, academic folklorists, and the literary establishment in general. Despite the book's solid and well-founded thesis, reviewers were put off by its angry tone and the author's tendency to lapse into snide remarks, bitter asides, personal opinions, and value judgments. Legman's inability to pander or compromise was coupled with a kind of obsessive chasing down of minutiae and an obstinate refusal to use footnotes for this pursuit. As a result, *Love & Death* was not really taken seriously by academic reviewers who had a difficult job accustoming themselves to its author's lively belligerence. Other readers, however, deeply appreciated Legman's special form of precocity and claimed that this was what made the book so compelling and rewarding. It was this same refusal to compromise that, according to John Clellon Holmes (1967), led Jay Landesman, reading through the draft manuscript of *Love & Death* for the first time, to declare in astonishment, "Good god, do you realize? I've met an honest man!" (p. 20).

Legman continued to publish widely during the next couple of years, including an article on David Ricardo and Ricardian theory (Franklin and Legman, 1949), articles on popular fiction, editorials in *Neurotica*, and lexicographical documentation on slang phrases in *American Speech*. By 1950, disappointed with the publisher's sales of *Love & Death*, he had started to distribute the book out of his own home in the Bronx, something that led to constant and extensive harassment by the Post Office due to the fact that the book contained a number of "obscene" words. An article titled "Notes on Masochism" originally intended for *Neurotica* No. 5 led to further irritation from the Post Office, and in the end the article was printed and circulated privately.

Also in 1950, Hamilton and Legman published a pamphlet titled *On the Cause of Homosexuality: Two Essays, the Second in Reply to the First*. In his essay, Legman made his feelings about homosexuality quite explicit for the first time: he endorsed an enthusiastically heterosexual stance and explained his conviction that homosexuality is a dangerous "perversion" that can be cured. Today, of course, this position is quite untenable. But it is important to remember that Legman was an American Jew who lived through the years of the Holocaust and a Freudian who regarded homosexuality as connected not to emancipation and liberation but to the violence and male aggression of Ernst Rohm and his Brownshirt thugs. A proponent of traditional psychoanalysis (which he tied very closely to his own zealous heterosexuality), Legman was deeply apprehensive of a sexual orientation that he associated with misogyny and brutality.

Critic Timothy Perper (January 18, 2003, personal communication) has speculated that Legman associated homosexuality with the homophilic bonding of some of the Nazis and its horrendous outcome. Similarly, Legman's friend Martha Cornog has suggested that, as a long-time champion of the love of women—their bodies, heterosexuality, and motherhood (and maybe a zero on the Kinsey Scale, that is, totally straight)— Legman associated heterosexuality and the love of women with birth and life and nature, and (male) homosexuality with sterility, death, and the worst of mechanized civilization and war. He also seemed to regard lesbianism as a rejection of birth (this was long before lesbian motherhood was more or less common), and a rejection of a partnership that can unite the best of male and female ideal types, each tempering the excesses and deficits of the other, to the benefit of the two parties and the benefit of human life.[5]

According to Davis (2002), in the early months of 1950, Legman received a letter from an official of the U.S. Post Office accusing him of retailing "indecent, vulgar and obscene materials" through the mails under the Fraud, Fictitious Business and Lotteries Statute. Not one to take such an accusation lying down, Legman requested a hearing with the Senior Trial Examiner of the U.S. Post Office to contest the finding. The hearing took place on June 6, 1950; a wheelchair-bound Legman (he had

---

[5] More recently, similar ideas were taken up by Klaus Theweleit (1987, 1989) in his studies of the Freikorps, a loosely knit fellowship of disaffiliated young men, many former soldiers, who gathered together after World War I to redeem the Fatherland's savaged honor in the context of what they perceived as the debasements of the Weimar Republic and the rising tide of Bolshevism. According to Theweleit, the Freikorps' murderous hatred of Communism was matched only by their murderous hatred of women's sexuality, one metaphorized and the other metonymized as the "Red Tide."

Theweleit uses Freikorps mores and costumes as a springboard for a masterful analysis of masculine anxiety surrounding castration and impotence, attendant terror of the feminine, and compensatory homosocial/homoerotic visions of male purity. This work has obvious, ominous currency regarding the contemporary American militia movement as well as other renascent fascist movements abroad. Recent studies extending Theweleit's interrogations of the "armored body" include Bukatman (1993) and Sharrett (1996).

broken his foot while trying to rescue a cat from his roof) defended himself in person, but unsuccessfully; his accusers informed him that not only were they keeping a close eye on his mail, but also he had earned himself an F.B.I. file.

It was Legman's ongoing conflict with the Post Office that finally led him to pack his books and leave the United States permanently. He sincerely believed, as did many other booksellers and publishers, that the Postmaster Generalship was the price the Democratic Party had paid for the political support of the Catholic Church. Catholic support was especially important to the Democratic Party since the urban working class, with its many immigrant Catholics, was a large voting block. A significant number of booksellers and publishers of erotica were the targets of fraud and obscenity prosecutions in the 1940s, and many believed that these arrests were the result of collaboration between the Post Office and the Catholic Legion of Decency—in return for Catholic political support.

A few months after Legman's hearing, the Post Office's complaint was upheld, and mail delivery stopped at 858 Hornaday Place. This meant that Legman could no longer receive answers to advertisements for *Love & Death*, and he had no way of getting the book out to potential buyers. This turn of events seemed to confirm his decision to opt out and finally leave the United States for good before he developed what he described to his friend Philip Kaplan as an "Ulcerus Americanus" (Legman to Philip Kaplan, March, 3, 1956, Philip Kaplan Collection); in 1953, he decided to move to Europe permanently.

He and his wife, Beverley, traveled initially to Paris, where Legman was overseeing the European publication of his book *The Limerick: 1700 Examples* (1953)—which could not be published in the United States at the time owing to its explicitly sexual content—on behalf of the publisher, Seymour Hacker. The couple lived in Paris for a few years and then began traveling around, looking for a place to settle more permanently. They arrived one day by train on the Riviera and, overwhelmed by the sight of the flowering bougainvillaea, decided to settle in the south of France. For around five years, they lived in various warm coastal towns, including Cagnes-sur-Mer and Auribeau, before finally settling in Valbonne, a small mountain village just outside Antibes in the Alpes Maritimes. Here, Legman bought a small, crumbling building—a ruined installation of the Knight's Templars known as La Clé des Champs—with an eye to restoration.

Gershon and Beverley quickly settled into their new home, which consisted of a small, moderately old two-room stone house with a separate building about 50 meters farther down the road that Legman made into his office. In this small studio, he installed his enormous library and collection of arcane erotica. He planned to pursue his research at the Bibliothèque Nationale in Paris and perhaps the British Museum in London. The property was surrounded by fields that in spring were full of wild flowers, and, as they had in the Bronx, Gershon and Beverley also quickly accumulated a large brood of stray cats.

From France, Legman continued to correspond with Kinsey and poke around for the occasional volume for him or point him in the direction of a book dealer; but the correspondence remained rather strained and formal, and the two men never returned to their earlier familiarity. In 1953, Legman published the results of his research on the limerick but, gun-shy from his earlier run-ins with the Post Office, issued the volume anonymously (though anybody in the know could easily recognize Legman's inimitable style). *The Limerick*, a massive collection of the world's dirtiest instances of that form, includes several original limericks by Legman, some acknowledged and some unacknowledged. In its introduction, *The Limerick* addresses a number of fascinating and complicated questions, explaining how and why limericks are written, why they seem to be so popular among English-speaking people, and why limericks are never written in languages other than English. Significantly, the book caught the attention of a psychology publisher in New York, Henry Schuman, who, deciding that Legman would be just the man to write a book on the general subject of dirty jokes, inspired him to start research on what would eventually become his most encyclopedic and notorious work, *Rationale of the Dirty Joke* (1968). A supplementary edition of *The Limerick*, full of new material, was later published under the title *The New Limerick* (1977a).

Among his many other accomplishments, Legman is also credited with having helped to introduce the art of origami to the West, and devoted much of these early years in France to his work on perfecting his techniques in this art. He had first been introduced to the pastime in

Scranton, Pennsylvania by a schoolmate, Cyril (who went on to become the film director Cy Endfield). Legman's specialty, unsurprisingly, was erotic paper-folding (see Legman, 1952a,b,c) and he developed a perfect design for "Lingam and Yoni" (Legman, 1952d). In 1955, he helped organize an origami exhibition at the Museum of Modern Art in Amsterdam, which was later brought to America. He also prepared a small book on the subject, which, because of disagreements with the publisher, never appeared. Belligerent conflicts are a recurrent theme in Legman's life; his blunt and aggressive personal manner meant that he was often unpopular, especially with those who did not understand or could not go along with his inability to affect a civil or courteous façade in their company. He even managed to fall out with the United States Origami Association, from which he resigned in anger over what John Vinocur (1975) described as a "dispute of Talmudic minuteness" over a badly bent corner (p. 96).

Alfred Kinsey's untimely death in 1956 was believed by many to be the result of his tendency to overwork, exacerbated by the pressure and outcry over the publication of the second Kinsey Report, *Sexual Behavior in the Human Female* (Kinsey, 1953).[6] Although Legman had been very critical of the first Kinsey Report, he was impressed by the second, and wrote to Paul Gebhard that he felt it avoided the "improper and tendentious statistical slanting" (Legman to Paul Gebhard, April 13, 1959, Alfred Kinsey Collection) of the original. "I liked the Female volume," he later wrote to Gebhard. He added cheekily that, as "Kinsey's official bibliographer," he would be happy to continue with his book buying work for the Institute. "My bibliographical knowledge on erotic subjects is, I may say in all modesty, unparalleled in the world at the present time," he boasted, "now that M. Louis Perceau is dead, and the bibliographers of the Bilder-Lexicon staff out of the field."

The shrewd Gebhard, however, had already glanced through the Legman-Kinsey correspondence and was understandably reluctant to engage Legman's book-buying expertise, at least initially. "My impres-

---

 [6] Legman claimed to fellow sexologist Clifford Scheiner that the final stroke that took Kinsey's life was occasioned by the mention of Legman's name; no evidence for this claim has been found.

sion," he responded honestly, "is that you are one of the world's leading authorities regarding erotic literature, and that you are a rather gifted writer, and that on occasion you can be untrustworthy and unscrupulous"—an impression which, he claimed, he had received from Kinsey, and which Kinsey "retained to the end of his life" (Legman to Paul Gebhard, May 1, 1959).

Legman, in turn, seemed to appreciate the frank openness of Gebhard's reply and tried to answer some part of it. In his response, defending his criticism of the first Kinsey Report, he pointed to the recent notoriety of Nabokov's *Lolita* ("a crappy pornographic novel published in Paris for the trade") and "the renaissance of homosexual literature since 1949" as evidence that "one of the principal things the public has absorbed from your activity is that 'Anything goes!'" (Legman to Paul Gebhard, May 5, 1959). The level-headed Gebhard took the criticism in good stead and continued to correspond with Legman on a friendly basis for many years. They met from time to time during his infrequent visits to the United States.

During the early 60s, Legman seemed to be growing increasingly annoyed about the way his work was ignored by those within the academic establishment. Part of this anger can be related to the fact that his projects at this time were more traditional than some of his earlier work and contained fewer of the bitter outbursts and sideswipes that characterized *Love & Death*. Perhaps he was taking his first genuine steps to be considered more seriously by the "official" folklorists, something that had always been hindered by his lack of formal academic training.

In 1961, he published a scholarly introduction to the anonymous erotic memoir *My Secret Life* (1961a) and wrote a review of Alan Lomax's *Folksongs of North America in the English Language* (1961b). In 1962, he published unexpurgated bibliographies of British and American folk ballads (1962a) and the preface to a bibliography of forbidden books (1962b); he edited and introduced a selection of the erotic and humorous songs of French medical students (1962c), and contributed a number of scholarly articles (1962d,e). In 1966, in addition to writing a scholarly introduction to the *Dictionary of Slang and Its Analogues* (1966a), he reviewed Alan Lomax's *Folksongs of North America in the*

English Language (1966b) and contributed a scholarly introduction to the anonymous erotic memoir *My Secret Life* (1966c).

Still he continued to work without university funding, without research grants, without photocopying facilities and without academic recognition—the last especially gradually became an issue of great acrimony to him, and he continued to write scornful passages of vitriol about "university professors," especially those in folklore departments. "I have never been able to bend the knee and lick the shoe properly, and so the foundation jobs and articles always go to someone else. How much work do I have to do, myself, before somebody gives *me* an honorary degree?" (Legman to Paul Gebhard, February, 10, 1961, Alfred Kinsey Collection).

And yet Legman was always his own worst enemy. Since he so often attacked scholarship with great wit and glee, it is little wonder he was never offered support, financial aid, or gratitude from "university professors," especially those in folklore departments. By writing the way he did, he often offended his academic peers with his bitter comments about the state of current sex and humor scholarship and his angry rants about corrupt professors who all seemed to be funding one another's pet projects. Perhaps what made most of his academic readers feel uncomfortable, however, was that Legman's scholarship was full of his own erratic consciousness—he abandoned the distance that most academic writers need, especially those involved in the study of sexuality, in order to make their discussions feel safe.

But it was a high price to pay. Legman often resorted to writing begging letters to colleagues in the United States—publishers, booksellers, and scholars who seemed sympathetic to his work. His situation was especially desperate in the spring of 1961, when lung cancer was diagnosed in Beverley, a lifelong heavy smoker. In April, he wrote, in a letter that was apparently typical of such requests at this time, to see if a colleague, Philip Kaplan, could send him some money:

We have already cut out everything possible: coffee, cigarettes, bread, everything. We now eat rice and our own home-grown tomatoes. We have no electricity, toilet, or any of that. And, my wife is sick. Can you loan me any money? It almost doesn't matter how much. Ten dollars will keep us alive nearly two weeks. A hundred or two hundred would see us through to November . . . Please help me [Legman to Philip Kaplan, April 14, 1961, Philip Kaplan Collection].

In 1963, Legman was invited to make his first tentative steps toward being embraced by the academic establishment. He was invited to give a series of lectures at the University of Ohio and then, at the invitation of the eminent folklorist Wayland Hand, to spend a year as scholar-in-residence at the University of California in La Jolla, where he taught classes on folklore. In November, he arrived in the United States for the first time since his self-imposed exile 10 years earlier. His complete isolation from contemporary social and political events is summed up by an anecdote he later told to John Vinocur (1975) about his arrival in the United States: "'I get off the boat on November 22, 1963, and the porter tells me, 'They've killed the President.' And I say, 'What would anyone want to shoot Eisenhower for?'" (p. 126).

One of his first stops was at the Origami Center in New York city, where he was the guest of honor at a special dinner party arranged by paperfolding enthusiast Lillian Oppenheimer for pioneers of the art. He went on to visit his academic colleagues, "all the courageous folklorists who were not scared to consider sexual folklore," he later recalled to Christine Hoffmann (Legman to Christine Hoffmann, February 9, 1976, Alfred Kinsey Collection). These included Christine's father, folklorist Frank Hoffmann, and his colleague Richard Dorson in Bloomington; scholars Herbert Halpert, D. K. Wilgus, and Wayland Hand; and a number of others. At the University of Ohio, he gave a lecture based on the ideas outlined in *Love & Death*, ideas that had gained much more currency during the turbulent decade of the 60s than when the book was first published. And it was during this lecture, according to reviewer R. Z. Sheppard (1975), that he came up with the slogan, "Make Love, Not War" (p. 96). This anecdote has never been confirmed, but two months later, Legman claims, he first began to see the words on students' lapel buttons around campus.

In general, however, neither his return to America nor his venture into the academic world was a success. During the time Legman had been living in France, in the late 50s and early 60s, the United States Supreme Court had made a series of landmark decisions that struck down antiobscenity statutes, inevitably opening the floodgates to the cheapest and most sordid kinds of commercial pornography. Unprepared for these changes and disturbed by what he saw as the mindless, drugged-out, anti-intellectualism of his students, Legman managed, as usual, to offend far more people than he impressed.

His principal subject was folklore, but his favorite activity seems to have been creating the Legend of Gershon Legman. "The kids would space out, disappear," he complained to Vinocur in 1975.

I used to burn bonfires of pot in a living-room grate. The campus was rotten with drugs. At one stage, I got banned from speaking to the students because I ran two courses called Orgasm I and Orgasm II. They were about literature. If it had been Violence I and II, there would have been no problem [p. 126].

It was not long before he was banned from teaching by the authorities, but, since he had an unbreakable one-year contract, he stayed on in La Jolla for two terms, making trouble. He attached a little bell to his lapel. "If any kid talked to me in the elevators," he recalled in an interview with Helen Dudar (1984), "I would shake it and say, 'Unclean! Unclean!'" (p. 42). He organized his followers into a group called the Hemlock Society and gave his courses outdoors, on the lawn. All he wanted to teach the students was nothing more dangerous, he told Dudar, than that "love is the thing that beats here in the chest, not here in the pants" (p. 42).[7]

Legman was appalled by the laid-back attitude of his pot-smoking Californian students, particularly their lack of engagement in any serious intellectual thought and their assumption that their behavior was some-

---

[7] Legman often dropped hints that he had "a freshman girl carpet" while at La Jolla, implying that he found it hard to shake off the attentions of fawning undergraduates. He refers to "married graduate instructors and young professors, to whom embarrassing numbers of coed girls regularly offer their Anatomical All along with their theme papers (this is *not* folklore)" (Legman, 1968, p. 521).

how revolutionary. Dope, group sex, and cheap pornography were not what Legman had spent his youth crusading for. His disgust was articulated in characteristically overheated prose in *The Fake Revolt* (Legman, 1967). The title of the book refers to the countercultural revolution of the 1960s, which Legman considered to be "fake" in comparison with the "real" student revolts in Paris. He despised hippies in particular, not for their pacifism or their belief in free love, but in their lack of passion or enthusiasm, their ostentatious display of "cool," which prevented the zealous expression of heterosexuality of which Legman was such a champion. Legman (1975) refers to "the inability to love" as "the curse of our century" (p. 740). "Cool," he writes in *The Fake Revolt*, "is the new venereal disease" (Legman, 1967, p. 12).[8]

The Fake Revolt is also, in part, an angry, blistering rant about the thoughtless popularity of drugs among young people in America. By means of his usual arrogant diatribes and fearless polemic, Legman makes some highly shrewd and prescient connections between drug use and the imperatives of American consumer culture in general: "Everybody's been turned in at least twice, including your local pot-pusher," he tells the parents of drug-using teenagers, "so put down that telephone":

> It isn't because the cops don't know *who he is* that your children are taking drugs. It's because *you* brought them up to be patsies for anything anybody offers them. "Tear off seven box-tops and the head of your mother, and you'll receive this wonderful plastic cape, as worn by Flying Crud." . . . remember? Now, when they offer them some other kind of crud, kids remember what you taught them (or allowed them to be taught by the "media"), and sop that up too [p. 25].

The effects of Legman's disastrous sojourn at La Jolla were long lasting. Frank Hoffmann, Legman's colleague and a folklorist at Indiana

---

[8] Legman's attitude toward sexuality, and his disillusionment with the hippie culture of the 60s and 70s, calls to mind the 30s work of Wilhelm Reich, such as *Mass Fascism* (1946) and *Function of the Orgasm* (1968), with which Legman was quite familiar.

University, was hoping to follow him to California the following year, also as scholar-in-residence. But, still recovering from their experience with Legman, the authorities at La Jolla made it clear that no more folklorists would find a place there (Hoffmann to Brottman, April 17, 2003, personal communication). To make things even worse, Legman had fallen out with the trustees of the Kinsey Institute after they refused, on the grounds that he was not considered to be "close enough" to the Institute, to send him photocopies of important erotic material he had been waiting for. "The fact of the matter is that I was 'close' to Kinsey before any of the three of you ever heard of him," wrote Legman with great indignation to Cornelia Christianson of the Kinsey Institute. "In fact, it is I who got the original penis measurements from him. . . . How much 'closer' would I have to be, to let Kinsey measure my penis?" (Legman to Cornelia Christianson, March 12, 1965, Alfred Kinsey Collection).

In 1964, while Legman was busy offending his colleagues at La Jolla, his new work was published, *The Horn Book: Studies in Erotic Folklore and Bibliography* (Legman, 1964a). This huge volume consisted of almost 600 pages devoted to outlining and analyzing the existing literature of erotic humor and folklore in the main European languages. Although a lot of this material had been published elsewhere, *The Horn Book* also contained much clever original work, including a discussion of bibliographical problems in the collecting of erotic literature; an introduction to Robert Burns's rediscovered manuscript *The Merry Muses of Caledonia;* and some thoughts about the etiology of the limerick. The book was praised with some reservations by Frank Hoffmann (1967) and more wholeheartedly by Alan Dundes (1965), who described it as a series of "masterfully written essays" and its author as "the James Joyce of folklore" (p. 161).

Legman's domestic arrangements often seemed to be something of a mystery to his friends and colleagues. Before leaving for La Jolla, he appears to have arranged for a separation—possibly even a divorce—from his wife Beverley. After his return to Europe, he wrote to Jay Landesman that "Beverley has been very sick, and sent me to America imagining she would die or something, for me to Begin Again. Otherwise I would never have gone. Now that I found out what's what, I am back, and all the divorcing and remarrying has been an absurdity" (Legman to Jay Landesman, July 14, 1965, Jay Landesman Papers). He brags rather implausibly to Landesman that in La Jolla, "as a single man in a college town full of father-complex kids . . . I had a wall-to-wall fresh-man girl carpet, and it nearly killed me."

At some point during his year in the United States, however, Legman was almost certainly married to a woman he met in New York named Christine Conrad; it was a marriage that was quickly annulled. Christine Conrad was, according to Legman, a beautiful, red-haired ex-Playboy Bunny with a degree in philosophy whom Legman apparently married on the spur of the moment after hearing her favorite dirty joke. His research on dirty jokes had led him to believe that women generally tell them only to telegraph their fears or to turn off would-be seducers, but the joke told to him by this unusual woman seemed to signal something totally different. The joke, according to Legman, went like this: A girl goes up to a boy at a party and says, "Want to fuck?" He answers, "Your place or mine?" The girl replies, "Well, if it's such a hassle for you, forget it." "Oh, the despair of that joke," exclaimed Legman to John Vinocur (1975). "I intuited at once that this woman couldn't bear the constant crude advances of the kind of man she had come into contact with night after night. Everything ended in disaster for her. What a challenge for me! . . . It was a crazy way to get married—one dirty joke out of 60,000—and it ended in divorce" (p. 126).

On his return to La Clé des Champs, Legman was faced with per-haps the most difficult 18 months of his life. When Beverley was taken into hospital—a public hospital, since the couple had no medical insur-ance—Gershon was left to look after the olive trees, feed the 17 cats they had accumulated (he didn't believe in spaying), and visit Beverley in hos-pital by bus (he never owned a car). He was also forced to sell off part of his priceless collection of erotica and folklore to pay for Beverley's med-ical treatments. She died at home in July, with her husband by her side.

Never one to be alone for long, on October 29, 1966, just three months after Beverley's death, Legman married Judith Evans, whom he described in a letter to colleague Bob Sewall as "a lovely Berkeley girl" (Legman to Bob Sewall, August 17, 1968, Philip Kaplan Collection). She was a children's librarian whose mother, Patricia Evans, was the author of a well-known children's rhyme book, *Rimbles*, and whose father was the floral artist Henry Evans. The marriage lasted until Legman's death in February 1999. Judith commented to obituarist Janny Scott after her husband's death that she was unsure whether their marriage was his second or third (p. 49); Legman told Vinocur (1975) that Judith was his "fourth" wife (p. 94) (perhaps following Beverley Keith, Christine Conrad, and Beverley Keith again). However, since Legman (1968) makes the claim that "monogamic marriage, as practiced in the west, is the principal focus of male sexual anxiety" (p. 23), it seems unlikely that any of Legman's marriages were of the traditional kind. When discussing his proposed memoirs with Landesman, he explained that he planned to end them with his marriage to Judith, since "nobody wants to read about a spouse's infidelities, even mental, which is why I refused to interview Linda Lovelace at Cannes: I knew the backers of the idea were setting it up for the historic meeting of Theory and Practice, and I did not think I wanted to expose Judith to such" (Legman to Jay Landesman, December 4, 1979, Jay Landesman Papers).

The same year that Beverley died and Legman remarried, he produced scholarly introductions to the already mentioned dictionary of slang (1966a), to an early collection of bawdy Russian folktales (1966b), and to the first successful edition of *My Secret Life* (1966c), a Victorian memoir concerned almost exclusively with its anonymous author's erotic experiences. He also published a study of heresy and sexual repression in the medieval order of the Knight's Templars (1966d), which deals with the question of whether charges of sodomy against the group were true or trumped up. Legman demonstrates how the so-called heresies of the Templars were related to the survival of certain practices in Gnostic, priapic, and witchcraft cults and to the political and economic policies of the order and the sexual hypocrisies of their time. The book got mixed reviews but was taken very seriously in academic journals like *Speculum* and *Journal for the Scientific Study of Religion*.

The year 1968 was an important one in Legman's life. Not only did it see the publication of his magnum opus, *Rationale of the Dirty Joke,* but his wife, Judith, gave birth to their first son, David Guy, whom he described in a letter to his friend Bob Sewall as "an enormous boy-hero weighing nearly 10 lb. at birth!" (Legman to Bob Sewall, August 17, 1968, Philip Kaplan Collection). In 1956, Legman had fathered an out-ofwedlock child, Ariela Legman. Ariela's Dutch mother was living in Amsterdam at the time, but neither Legman nor his first wife was especially interested in raising children. Judith, however, was significantly younger than her husband, who was now approaching 50, and Legman had changed his mind about having children after his visit to the U.S. in 1964. In America, as he wrote to Christine Hoffmann, he discovered that the "courageous folklorists" with whom he was staying "all seemed to have young children or teen-agers," and being around these agreeable youngsters—"the folklore kids," as Legman called them—played a big part in his decision to have children of his own at last (Legman to Christine Hoffmann, February 9, 1976, Alfred Kinsey Collection).

The following year, 1969, saw an elegant reprint of Legman's (1940) first book, *Oragenitalism*. The first volume had been devoted solely to "Cunnilinctus"; this expanded volume, published almost 30 years later, took advantage of the new climate of sexual freedom to include sections on "Fellation," "Irrumation," and "Soixante-Neuf." Legman was very proud of this work, which he claimed to be the earliest book of its kind and, at least for many years, the only one. Reviewers of this new edition, however, especially in the more sexually conservative climate of Britain, found it hard to keep from tittering. John Coleman (1972) described the book with a snigger as "the last tongue-in-cheek word on oral-genital contacts." He continued:

> Mr. Legman's intentions are clearly genuine, to promote the maximum exploration of our possibilities for sexual enjoyment, and he keeps an amazingly straight face while proposing such subtleties as the "Bowling-Hold" and the "Candy Bar." He warns against waxed and pointed moustaches and uses the word "pudibundity" rather a lot. A man's man, he also seems tetchy about the implied passivity of cunnilinctus and fellation, opting for the more dominant activity of irrumation. Anyone concerned to enlarge his sexual vocabulary will find Mr. Legman a boon [pp. 180–181].

Partly as a result of such reviews, Legman began to achieve further notoriety in the underworld of "gallantiana." For example, in Nicholas Schors's *Memoirs of an Erotic Bookseller*, published under the pseudonym Armand

Legman and family in France, 1975
(photographs by Bruce Jackson and
John Waggaman)

Coppens (1969), Legman has a cameo appearance as "that vain genius . . . with the thing about dirty limericks and four-letter words" (p. 86).

But the vain genius was having some serious health problems; his correspondence during 1971 is full of references to his failing eyesight. "I am arranging to sell a large portion of my library by private treaty," he wrote to Philip Kaplan in September of that year, "owing to a great need for money for specialists as to my eyesight" (Legman to Philip Kaplan, September 27, 1971, Philip Kaplan Collection). In another letter to Kaplan in November, dictated to Judith, Legman asks to be sent some classical music records to listen to, "anything from Bach through Beethoven (I mean chronologically: the later Romantics get me all nervous and it breaks the little capillaries in my eyes); I could now use them prayerfully" (Legman to Philip Kaplan, November 28, 1971, Philip Kaplan Collection).

Over the next three years, Judith gave birth to two more children; another boy, Rafael, was born in 1971, and a girl, Sara Felicity, in 1973. Throughout the 70s, the Legmans happily welcomed any interested colleagues willing to make the trip to France. They were visited by, among others, Norman Mailer, accompanied by an early wife and a lesbian poet, who came expecting a series of swinging orgies, only to discover that Legman, although joyously sexual, was no longer sexually adventurous. Others who made the trip to Valbonne during the 70s include the noted sexologists Ira Reiss and Clifford Scheiner; American Studies professor Bruce Jackson; his wife, the English professor Diane R. Christian; and the humor scholar Victor Raskin.

Although Legman developed something of a public reputation for surliness and belligerence, many of those who knew him in person describe him as generous to a fault. These include Martha Cornog, a young woman who originally began corresponding with Legman on the subject of origami and who eventually became interested in the study of sexuality (she later recruited him to contribute a chapter on erotic bibliography to her book *Libraries, Erotica and Pornography* [Legman, 1991]). Cornog corresponded with Legman for 30 years, and, in an article written shortly after Legman's death (Cornog and Perper, 1999), recalls her amazement at "his and Judith's willingness to write reams of long and serious letters—and to send free books—to an unknown young woman struggling with intellectual and personal curiosities" (pp. 316–317).

Another scholar with fond memories of Legman's patient support is Patrick Kearney, author of *The Private Case*—a catalogue of the erotica kept in the British Library—for which Legman (1981) contributed a splendid introduction. According to Kearney, Legman read through the proofs of the manuscript, made numerous suggestions for notes and revisions, and was always ready with information and encouragement (Kearney to Brottman, May 31, 2003, personal communication). In fact, it was Legman who was responsible for getting *The Private Case* published in the first place. He brought it to the attention of Jay Landesman, who agreed to publish the manuscript—quite a serious undertaking, especially for such a small press.

In 1975, in connection with some advance publicity arranged by the publishers of the forthcoming second volume of the *Rationale*, Legman was visited by John Vinocur (1975), the American journalist who had been sent to interview him for a profile in *Oui* magazine—"the glossy magazine of 'hip' sexual perversion," as Legman (1975) refers to it (p. 380). The resulting article (Vinocur, 1975) is rather bitchy and full of gossipy details. The first paragraph captures the tone nicely:

> "You goddam *Time* guys, you're all alike in your blue shirts," Gershon Legman is complaining. "Praising Marlon Brando. The primitive. A man of culture does not fuck a woman up the ass, I don't care what the script says."[9] I remind him that I'm from *Oui*, not *Time*, but he doesn't care. Irritation has set in and he's into a supersulk. Crossing one leg of sloppy white duck over the other, scratching at the white stubble on his face and pulling his Wonder Warthog T-shirt down over two and a half ripples of pre-cardiac gut, Legman looks like an irritated baker on a cigarette break. Can this be the world's greatest scholar of the dirty joke? [pp. 94–96; 126–128].

---

[9] For some reason, Legman had an irrational hatred of Marlon Brando, expressed on numerous occasions. "I walked out of *Last Tango in Paris*." he told Vinocur (1975). "I find anal intercourse dirty and unpleasant" (p. 126).

Vinocur describes Legman as "testy and lively" and his conversation as full of "free-associative rushes" about his childhood in Scranton. He speaks of Legman's squabble with the American Origami Association and his quarrel with Henry Schuman, the New York publisher who originally commissioned *Rationale of the Dirty Joke*. When Vinocur drove Legman into the village for lunch, Legman ordered a plate of steak and rice and continued his stream of disconnected conversation, discoursing freely on subjects as varied as the calendar riots of 1742, Samuel Pepys, the vocabulary of seduction, and his own abortive marriage to Christine Conrad, the "Playboy Bunny with a philosophy degree," as he always referred to her.

Back in the studio that afternoon, the talk turns to the forthcoming book, and Legman grows irritated with Vinocur's attempts to get him to tell a dirty joke. "He announces that my nosy questions and the general pain I am giving him in the intellectual ass have necessitated a little glycerin pickup for his heart," writes Vinocur. And when the interviewer suggests that it might be fun to write up a list of the world's 20 most offensive dirty jokes, Legman becomes choleric. "'I'm a scholar,' he says, almost shouting. 'I'm not a gangster of the New Freedom who fucks girls in the ass and screams, 'New Freedom, New Freedom.' I will not participate in this kind of scheme" (p. 126).

The resulting article makes Legman out to be hostile, belligerent, eccentric, verbose, and bad tempered, by turns arrogant and irritable, ridiculous, and somewhat pathetic in appearance. Legman (1975), however, takes his revenge in *No Laughing Matter*, where he presents his own version of Vinocur's visit:

He hunched over a small table, flipping the pages and feverishly writing down the jokes (only), while I tried to indicate to him some of the subjects of the accompanying text; mentioning . . . that some people even like—or at least tell—jokes on such subjects as vomit, nasal mucus, "toe-punk," and preputial smegma. He looked at me with an air of intense expectation, the way Balboa must have looked when he first sighted the Pacific. "Mr. Legman!," he pleaded, gripping both legs of the table, "Tell me a joke! Tell me a joke about SMEGNA!" As I observed he couldn't even pronounce it, I figured he probably couldn't spell it, and was mean enough to refuse. He revenged himself in a hilariously offensive smear-piece . . . noting severely that I look "like an exhausted wart-hog" and am hung up on the subject of homosexuality in jokes—which nobody can deny [p. 380].

The New Limerick: 2750 Unpublished Examples: American and British (Legman, 1977a) was published as a supplement to Legman's (1953) volume, *The Limerick*. This second volume contains an extensive bibliography of limerick collections, a new chapter on science-fiction limericks, and a discussion of foreign-language "equivalents" to the limerick and of the main printed collections of these. In the book's revised introduction, Legman analyzes the appeal of the limerick along the same lines as his analysis of the appeal of the dirty joke. He explains how "the screen-concentration on the personal or geographical name ending the first line of the limerick" (p. xvii) provides an ego-assuaging mask in which "we blurt out our deepest-hidden secrets and unveil our most private fears, fancies, and imagined deficiencies in doggerel rhyme, under the satirical mask of each other's names" (p. xviii). "Who are limericks really about but ourselves?" asks Legman. "Who, really, are the impossible idiots and unavowable perverts whose anatomical anomalies and erotic peculiarities are the inexhaustible subject of all this doggerel humor?" (p. xix):

> The question obviously answers itself. Limericks are the tragicomic autobiographies of the Pagliaccis who write and recite them. They are . . . little thumbnail autobiographies, stripping some little human tragedy naked in five lines, under the paperthin disguise of exaggerated verbal humor and rhyme. . . . You hold the mask of laughter over my name and my unavowably shameful face, and I will hold the mask over yours [p. xix].

Bruce Jackson (1980) reviewed *The New Limerick* in glowing terms. He praised Legman's "serious and scholarly approach" and added that "he has tried to present in the two volumes as enormous a collection as anyone has ever dared present, and his introductions and notes try to make sense of that incredible mass of bizarre encounters and interlocked organs"

(p. 209). In 1977, Legman had become associated with a new journal, *Maledicta: The Journal of Verbal Aggression*, in whose first volume he published the first part of a study of witty obscenities and colorful turns of phrase (Legman, 1977b) as well as a translation of an article on "Italian and Venetian Profundity" by G. Averna (Legman, 1977c). The third issue of *Maledicta*, in fact, was a *Festschrift* dedicated to Legman's work.

Legman had experienced trouble with an arrhythmic heartbeat for many years; this got much worse as he entered his 60s. "Two nights ago," he wrote to Jay Landesman on June 1, 1981, "after a perhaps excessive sexual effort at midnight, my heart stopped pumping, I began coughing, and was suddenly entirely unable to breathe: an intensely frightening situation, of strangling . . . I was positive it was all over with me" (Legman to Jay Landesman, July 30, 1987, Jay Landesman Papers). He recovered after the administration of oxygen, but his heart remained troublesome, as did his eyesight, which had been weak for a long time. Around this time, he traveled to the United States for a health check-up, to visit his mother, and to take an appalled look at the flowering of peepshows and dirty bookstores along 42nd Street. He had dreamt of happy, guiltless sex as a liberating force; instead, he discovered it had become an empty, meaningless opiate. In 1984, he claimed in an interview with Helen Dudar that "the worst part is the perversion of the love stuff":

> In the 30s we all believed that if we put our shoulder to the wheel, we'd progress, the world would change. There would be a new dawn, a new tomorrow. Today, nobody believes it. The hope is gone. Everything has been perverted and made into a business, rottenified. Love isn't going to liberate people. They aren't going to be liberated. That's the hard pill to swallow. There's no question of personal victory or nonvictory. The only victory I ever had is that I invented the vibrating dildo. That's my gift to humanity [p. 43].

Legman's claim to have invented the vibrating dildo, like his claim to have invented the slogan "Make Love, Not War," is difficult to verify.

Throughout the 1980s, he corresponded regularly and at some length with his old friend Jay Landesman and often waxed a little nostalgic about the way things might have been. The two were both at work on their memoirs,[10] and Legman wanted to be sure that their recollections of certain important events and episodes from the *Neurotica* days remained consistent. Throughout these letters, he refers from time to time to his old girlfriend Louise or "Beka" Doherty, a researcher for *Time* magazine, whom he remembers with great fondness and sentiment. He describes her to Landesman as "one of the two women I really should have married, and we both knew it" (Jay Landesman Papers, 1983).

In a later letter to Landesman, he seems to be referring again to Beka Doherty when he mentions a former girlfriend—"the one I had the greatest affair of my life with"—and wishes he had married her before she married someone else ("—then I should have lived a happy life instead of the life I lived!—" [Legman to Jay Landesman, August 17, 1989]). Chapter 54 in his unpublished memoir, "Peregrine Penis: An Autobiography of Innocence," was to have been titled "Louise," and, in fact, it was Beka Doherty who inspired the memoir's title. "Peregrine Penis," explains Legman to Landesman in a letter of July 30, 1987, was "a nickname that great Beka Doherty girl you mention gave me, when I used to travel to meet her in strange places" (Legman to Jay Landesman, July 30, 1987).

When French women began to go topless, Legman had to stop visiting the beach; he was put to flight not by the desensitizing presence of acres of assorted breasts, but by the fact that the occasional sight of a perfect pair was too much for him. At the age of 65, his heart had made sexual activity very difficult. "I now faint at orgasm," he confessed to Helen Dudar (1984), sadly. In 1986, he returned to the United States for the last time for a lecture tour and spent a few days with the editor of *Maledicta*, Reinhold Aman. He also attended a festive *Maledicta* party, to which people had traveled from all over the United States to meet him and that went on well into the early hours of the morning. After his stay with Aman in Wisconsin, he visited Bruce Jackson in Buffalo, New York; he also gave the keynote speech at the Annual Conference for the Association for the Study of Play in Tempe, Arizona. In 1992, his last sig-

---

10   Landesman's memoir was eventually published in 1987 as *Rebel Without Applause*. Legman's unfinished memoir, "Peregrine Penis," is currently being edited by his widow, Judith.

nificant project, *"Unprintable" Ozark Folksongs and Folklore*, was published. Comprising two massive volumes, it was based on the folk songs collected by Vance Rudolph in the Ozark mountains in Missouri, Illinois, and Arkansas, but omitted from his published edition (Rudolph and Legman, 1992).

Gershon Legman died in hospital on Tuesday, February 23, 1999, in Valbonne, after suffering a massive stroke the previous Saturday. A private funeral was held locally on Saturday, February 27. Legman (1975) had discussed the function of "ritual obscenity at funerals and wakes" (p. 742), but his own funeral was a very dignified affair. Legman's memoir of his sex life, "Peregrine Penis," remains unpublished.

Today, Gershon Legman remains a somewhat notorious figure in the narrow world of erotic folklore and bibliography, but the range and scope of his scholarship were never limited to any particular subject or field of study. His essays deal with everything that matters to human consciousness—social and cultural values, the state of civilization, philosophy, morality, and what it means to be human. He uses erotic writing and erotic literature as a springboard from which to launch into a series of deeply perceptive, emotional, spirited analyses of cultural history. His work goes far beyond the conventional boundaries of academic scholarship and takes for granted that such boundaries are random, artificial, and ultimately self-serving. For Legman, everything is connected, everything counts. In the end, he explains, all aspects of human civilization—moral, ethical, social and cultural—come down to the central truths of the body, of which the most essential of all is the emotion of physical love.

Interestingly, Legman finally admitted to Helen Dudar (1984) that he didn't like jokes at all. "After they get that first nervous laugh, they're depressing," he confessed. "I'm a poor raconteur and I never laugh. Maybe a little titsatibitsa laugh, but yokchatabotcha—hah hah hah—no" (p. 128).

CHAPTER 2

Against Jokes

Why do you laugh? Change the names, and the tale is told of you.

—Horace, *Satires* I.i.69

A man goes to the rabbi and says he wants to divorce his wife "because she has such filthy habits." "What are these habits?" asks the rabbi.

"Oh, I can't tell you," says the man. "It's too filthy to describe."

The rabbi refuses, under the circumstances, to grant him the divorce.

"Well, if I must, I must," says the man. "Every time I go to take a piss in the sink, it's always full of dirty dishes."

An innocent crack at marriage? According to Legman, no crack is ever innocent. This particular joke was told to him, he claims, in his hometown of Scranton, Pennsylvania, in 1936 by "a very respectable Jewish woman of middle age," and—like all jokes, believes Legman—has everything to do with the personal neuroses and proclivities of its teller. "Other than the obvious level of self-unveiling here, of the woman's unhappiness with her brutal and egoistic husband," argues Legman (1968), "there is perhaps a further level, even better concealed, in which the joke complains of women's woes concerning the household chores that make her too tired and unready to enjoy her sexual life, here alluded to in almost infantile terms, as 'pissing in the sink'" (p. 17).

Strongly influenced by Freud's work on jokes, Legman believed that humor and sex are completely inseparable. He made a good case for the argument that a person's sexual preferences and anxieties show themselves in the thinly disguised form of a favorite dirty joke. Legman (1975) contends that jokes carry a powerful clue to the teller's own psychological inclinations, tendencies that, by telling the joke, the teller is actually struggling to unveil, despite himself. "Your favorite joke is your psychological signature" (p.13), writes Legman. And everybody has a favorite. "It's precisely in these favorites of every joke-teller's, in his or her special repertory, that we may discern the face hidden behind the mask" (p. 14).

After browsing through the first volume of Legman's (1968) *Rationale of the Dirty Joke*, a friend of mine commented that Legman's analysis tended to "ruin the jokes." People often make the same kind of complaints about Freud's (1905) paper on jokes. Where are the funny parts? Since the point of both books is to explain that the whole process of joke telling is pathological, this seems a bit like complaining that knowing the plane is about to crash ruins your enjoyment of the in-flight movie. The truth is, knowing what is *really* going on during the joking process makes it almost impossible to enjoy another joke again, unless you are either extremely masochistic or in a process of deep denial.

A frequent complaint seems to be that to formulate a "science" of jokes drives out the capacity to laugh. Journalists reporting on conferences of humor scholars love nothing more than to point out what a dull and dry lot they all are—and if pictures can be snapped of any of them snoozing and drooling in their seats during the convention, all the better. A photo of two humor scholars who dozed off during a "Humor and Laughter" conference in Wales, for example, was published in *Time* magazine, along with Robert Benchley's observation that "there seems to be no length to which humorless people will not go to analyze humor" (Byron, 1976, p. 44).

Scholars of humor often respond to this accusation by claiming that to understand the psychodynamics of joke telling on a theoretical level should not prevent one from enjoying those same jokes on another, more visceral level, just as a gynecologist can still enjoy making love to his wife when he gets home. But what if the gynecologist were to discover that the internal organs of all women were horribly diseased? Would he still want to make love to his wife? If so, there would be something deeply wrong with him.

Once we have really absorbed what is at stake in the joking process, we *should* be troubled and haunted by it; we *should* end up, like Legman, being completely unable to laugh. The astute philosopher Max Eastman (1938) began with a combined warning and apology to the reader, with which I can only concur:

> I must warn you, reader, that it is not the purpose of this book to make you laugh. As you know, nothing kills the laugh quicker than to explain a joke. I intend to explain all jokes, and the proper and logical outcome will be, not only that you will not laugh now, but that you will never laugh again. So prepare for the descending gloom [p. 1].

And, though it may be of little consolation, I would add that nothing is more important than the capacity for self-knowledge and that disillusion is perhaps the most difficult and rewarding part of understanding the human condition.

Freud (1905) made the controversial observation that jokes are a socially acceptable way to express what otherwise cannot be said openly. He argued that, while there is a relief to be derived from expressing concealed truths, this relief occurs, paradoxically, because we laugh at that which makes us most anxious. Consequently, Freud argued, most wit is either hostile (serving as aggression, satire, or defense), or obscene (serving as sexual exhibition). "One gets the impression," argued Freud, "that the subjective determination of wit production is oftentimes not unrelated to persons suffering from neurotic disease" (p. 21).

The practical use of these ideas was first taken up after Freud's death by the Freudian analyst Israel Zwerling (1955), a great advocate of the diagnostic use of jokes in therapy. Zwerling emphasized that jokes are linked to the ideas and experiences that cause the greatest anxiety, at least covertly, to tellers and listeners alike (pp. 104–115). Many scholars of psychoanalysis have commented on the relationship between jokes and personality, and between the jokes someone tells and that person's current emotional situation. For example, psychoanalyst Ernst Kris (1940) wrote of laughter as a bodily process whose energy would otherwise be directed to safeguard adult behavior, so the telling of a joke affects the listener as an invitation to common aggression and common regression.

And as the audience of any nightclub comedy act can testify, the stronger the group spirit, the less effort is required to create laughter. Philosopher Peter Kivy (2003) describes this dynamic as "drawing the wagons into a circle" (p. 9), leaving those on the outside feeling lonely, left out, and repulsed. "Laughter," according to Kivy, "is a threatening snarl to the outsiders" (p. 8).

Of course, there has been a huge shift in psychoanalytic work and theory in the last 50 years, and Freud's ideas about humor no longer hold the currency they once did. Contemporary humor theorists now consider the subject from a variety of angles and from the perspective of more than 20 disciplines, including biology, philosophy, psychology, cultural studies, folklore, and linguistics. Most of these scholars give a warm, good-natured cast to the telling of jokes, without the nastiness and aggression that Legman—and, indeed, Freud—regard as an integral part of the joke-telling enterprise. Most would perhaps agree with philosopher Ted Cohen (1999), who makes the case, in a Kantian vein, that a successful joke brings us to the recognition of our common humanity. As he puts it,

> I need reassurance that this something inside me, this something that is tickled by a joke, is indeed something that constitutes an element of my humanity. I discover something of what it is to be a human being by finding this thing in me, and then having it echoed in you, another human being [p. 31].

To Legman, however, jokes are too bound up with aggression and anxiety to reveal anything pleasing about a common humanity. Legman was deeply grounded in Freudian theory and could not consider jokes as anything other than neurotic and confessional—a perspective that many contemporary humor theorists seem to find too unfashionable or disturbing to contemplate. "People do not joke about what makes them happy or what is sacred to them," wrote Legman (1968). "They joke only about what frightens or disturbs them, or about the pinnacles of happiness they would like to have scaled but failed at" (p. 44). In 1968, this provoking theory was elaborated at enormous length in the first volume of what was to become Legman's magnum opus, *Rationale of the Dirty Joke: An Analysis of Sexual Humor*, a work he had been preparing for more than 30 years. This huge volume of over 800 pages contains more than 2000 jokes and has since been reprinted twice in paperback, and translated into German, French, and Italian.

Legman claims in the book that his undertaking was partly inspired by Victor Hugo's (1869) masterpiece, *The Man Who Laughs*. For his epigraph, he took a line from Beaumarchais's *Figaro:* "I laugh, so that I may not cry."

As that telling inscription suggests, the *Rationale* is a very unfunny book, one certainly not intended as a compendium of dirty jokes to be brought out at stag parties or kept handy by the toilet. Instead, it illustrates that jokes are seldom "new" or "invented," but all relate to variants that have evolved from other times and civilizations, many being traceable to the Renaissance or earlier, appearing in the works of Boccaccio, Apuleius, and other tale-tellers. All jokes, writes Legman (1968), "arrive to us from other countries and older civilizations, by way of oral and printed infiltrations over a period of centuries, and along certain massive and well-deliniated cultural highways" (p. 34).

Emphasizing the connections between dirty jokes, laughter, and folklore, he deduces from the timeless popularity of such jokes, and their geographical ubiquity, that they are essentially important attempts to allay or express human fears and anxieties about sex and to project these fears and anxieties on to others. He goes on to argue that dirty jokes spring from unconscious fears and rages that are practically universal, although they tend to manifest themselves more often in males than in females. In fact, according to Legman, the telling of dirty jokes is often a kind of erotic approach to women, in which the male nudges some nonsexual remark of a woman's "into presumable sexual allusion," (p. 337), although, as Legman reminds us, "the punning importation of a sexual proposition into something that the man has said is used far more often for purposes of rejecting the fictitious proposition angrily than accepting it" (p. 340).

Freud (1905) suggested that jokes verbalize male aggressive instincts against the opposite sex, by whom they are simultaneously aroused and disturbed. Legman extends and embellishes Freud's basic theory into a strongly argued and compelling thesis. Jokes, especially dirty jokes, according to Legman's analysis, are always the expression of id impulses and not of the superego. "It may be stated axiomatically," writes Legman (1968), "that a person's favorite joke is a key to that person's character, a rule of thumb all the more invariable in the case of highly neurotic persons. In other words, the *only* joke you know how to tell is *you*." (p. 16).

Legman argues that all jokes are aggressive in nature, and dirty jokes in particular, generally told by males about females, are a vehicle by which men express their hostility toward women. Such jokes, according to Legman, deal with a highly charged neurotic situation in which the originator or the teller of the joke has been forced to live, and the function of humor in general is to reconcile us to the painful, unacceptable, or tragic aspects of the human condition. The telling of the joke thereby permits a "moral vacation" (p. 743) of uncontrolled hostility; the laughter aroused by jokes, if any, is less often of amusement than of relief, "when the ordeal of listening is over" (p. 38).

Rationale of the Dirty Joke makes for a fascinating and disturbing read. It is certainly enough to make anybody wary of telling any more dirty jokes, or even listening to them—and not just because any joke seems tame and redundant after one has ploughed through Legman's exhaustive anthology of examples. The *Rationale* makes the very notion of joke telling seem like a miserable and pathetic exercise, especially if we accept the premise that our taste in humor is the key to the depth of our anxieties, particularly regarding sex. "One of the most effective antidotes to fear is laughter," wrote an anonymous (1969) reviewer for *Time* magazine, "and man has been guffawing for years at fears of his own sexual inadequacy" (p. 43).

All dirty jokes, according to Legman, deal with sexual taboos that can be transgressed with impunity only in the form of humor. Often, the mere mention of the taboo word or act is enough to create the impression of a joke, since, of course, it would be unnecessary (as Freud [1913] said of incest) to forbid that to which no one is attracted. Legman goes on to discuss how relatively few actors are introduced into dirty jokes. As in all jokes, most of the figures they involve are "visibly stock characters rather than real people: men, women—husbands, lovers, wives, and prostitutes—parents and children, doctors, policemen, animals, fools" (p. 398).

Legman (1968) divides sets of jokes according to theme—the jokes are printed separately and in italics so they can be picked out easily— and then he discusses the various unconscious impulses that lead us to tell them. As usual, his intuitive ability to discern the psychological or neurotic endpoint of the jokes he discusses is uncannily perceptive. According to Legman, jokes testifying to a masochistic tendency include those in which the butt or the victim is the joker himself ("I've got a good joke on old Olly. He pays my wife $5.00 to fuck her, and I fuck her for nothing"). Legman points out that many Jewish jokes are of this kind, and he makes the interesting point that the material on which Freud (1905) based his *Jokes and Their Relation to the Unconscious* is also full of this kind of self-deprecating humor.

Sadistic jokes include those in which the listener is made the victim by being tantalized into expecting a point or denouement that doesn't exist, as in the shaggy dog story, which plays entirely on the listener's nervous expectations and unconscious involvement. Jokes about enormous penises are also sadistic—an extension (if you will) of the folkloric notion of the penis as a weapon that harms and may even destroy the woman.

Jokes told at the expense of ethnic or racial groups are actually jokes about comic versions of ourselves, seen through the distorting lens of a funhouse mirror. These kinds of jokes always tend to proliferate in periods of increasing political tension—consider the rash of anti-Arab jokes that circulated within days of the collapse of the World Trade Center. Such jokes are related to the spate of so-called sick jokes that tend to circulate soon after a major disaster or catastrophe. Legman explains that such jokes involve a conspicuous underreaction to the event, a reaction that, he claims, "is very appealing to the modern alienated personality which finds itself unable to react, especially with the demanded emotions of love or concern, and therefore welcomes the excuse of 'nonsense' to explain its emotional deadness" (p. 471).

Similarly, jokes about animals obviously represent humans through analogy. Legman reminds us of the story of David and Uriah's wife, represented to David by the prophet Nathan as a parable concerning "one little ewe lamb" (2. *Samuel*, xii, 1–9), in which "the repressed intention finally bursts through at the end of the story . . . with the prophet Nathan's bold *de te fabula narratur*: 'Thou art the man!'" (p. 191). Jokes about sexual orgies involving more than one male reveal, at least according to Legman, a conspicuous interest in disguised homosexual activity, "with the woman simply used as a pretext or coupling-joint" (p. 409).[1] Dirty jokes involving religious figures are often simple mockery of the antisexual pretensions of many Christian sects (p. 502).

Jokes about men who are irrationally fastidious about their sexual tastes, or men who can't find what they are looking for in a thousand woman, are interpreted as being essentially homosexual in theme, as are jokes about adultery. There is, claims Legman, an understood link between the cuckolded husband and his wife's traducer in the familiar story about the wife who admits to adultery while her husband was out of town (Husband: "Who was it, Finkelstein?" Wife: "No." "Cohen?" "No." "Shapiro?" "No." "What's the matter—none of my friends are good enough for you?"). Concludes Legman, "In the relationship with the other man that is crucial to adultery, it is the triumph over him, rather than the sexual conquest of his wife, that is understood to be the adulterer's real thrill" (p. 502). Interestingly, adultery shares this formal dynamic in common with joke-telling: the aim of both activities, if Legman is correct, is to make an impression on a triangulated, absent third figure.

Jokes about sexual organs that are either too large or two small in relation to their opposite number, and that make coupling impossible, are understood to express fears about temperamental incompatibility. Here they amplify the suppressed or merely tacit mismatched qualities and dispositions of many "ordinary" married couples: She: "It was all right, but I can't say I thought much of your organ." He: "No? Well, I didn't expect to play in an auditorium." Legman explains that jokes concerning the size of the female genitals represent a much more direct expression of anxieties than do similar jokes about the size of the penis,

---

[1] Legman (1968) has much to say about the individual's need for the strength and public permissiveness of the group (see, e.g., p. 520).

which generally imply a solution to the problem of genital mismatching "by fantastic and improbable means" (p. 377). Jokes about the size of the female genitals are countered by other jokes whose logic follows the folkloric male assumption—clearly intended to divert anxiety through a process of sympathetic magic—that women delight in absorbing any kind of penis at all, however small.

If these jokes about mismatched couples really have any surface meaning at all, explains Legman, "it is in connection with married hate and old age" (p. 539).[2] Even when jokes about marriage are not obviously hostile, they often contain a tone of force and violence, if not actual sadism. Legman remarks that there is "an additional or substitutive sexual pleasure rising from the violence or cruelty itself" (p. 664), a point he connects to Freud's observation that it is not our hatred for our enemies that harms us, but our hatred for the people we really love—a wonderful example of what Freud (1909) called the ambivalence of opposites.

Castration jokes, like vagina dentata stories, are told to reassure both teller and listener that these horrible things, though they may happen, happen only to somebody else. Jokes about bodily dissolution (wooden legs, blindness, and other mutilations) are obvious surrogates of castration, often projected on to the woman. Jokes about women ever-ready to be raped (and to love every minute of it) are a fantasy escape by men from the rigorous fidelity demanded of women in patriarchal societies.

Potency jokes, whose premise is that coitus is more important than anything else in the world, and jokes that assume all women are available as partners invariably conceal fears of inadequacy, rejection, or impotence. As Legman explains, since nobody can be quite as potent as the potency joke pretends, its final meaning is evidently a denial of fears of impotence, or of the inability to love or to satisfy a woman, or even to satisfy oneself (p. 313). Other categories in this volume, which limits itself to "clean" dirty jokes, include Children, Fools, Animals, The Male Approach, The Sadistic Concept, Women, Premarital Sexual Acts, and Marriage. The really "dirty" dirty jokes are reserved for the second volume.

---

2 Legman (1968) adds that "there is a natural element in this, of dominant maleness, but it cannot be pushed very far without becoming evident sex hate" (p. 664).

Interestingly, it is difficult to get very far into Legman's work without stopping to consider just *why* there are so many dirty jokes. As his encyclopedic collection of examples makes clear, dirty jokes are ubiquitous, but this does not necessarily mean that sex is particularly funny; indeed, most people would agree that sex and humor make uneasy partners. Many of us feel that, when we are right in the middle of a sexual act, nothing could be more serious. Lovemaking, as many have testified, is no laughing matter. A stifled giggle, a misplaced titter, a badly timed snicker—and everything is lost. Other expressions of emotion are acceptable in the bedroom and can even seem arousing. Shame, for example, can often be an aphrodisiac; bashful blushing can be a real turn on; anger can be erotic—especially the hot-tempered quarrel that leads to make-up sex. Even misery and regret can be sexy; many women, and even some men, shed a tear or two upon orgasm. Smiles of joy and affection are welcome, but hardly ever laughter.

Nevertheless, many people have observed that there is something inherently ridiculous, even comical, about human bodies observed in the strange act of copulation. What could be more absurd than the naked human body grunting, twitching, and sweating, legs astride, arms askew, buttocks humping and heaving? Imagine seeing the act of lovemaking from the point of view of a child, a eunuch, or an alien from another planet. Here are two naked adults contorting themselves into a series of grotesque positions and making all kinds of strange noises in the quest of a brief spasm in the genital region. What could be more preposterous?

Of course, we seldom think about sex in these terms. If we did, we would hardly ever be able to do it. Making love, it seems, is very much like driving, or dancing, or playing the piano: it is one of those automatic things that we can do properly only if we don't really concentrate on it at all. To enjoy ourselves sexually, we have to be completely engrossed in the act, both physically and mentally—so engrossed, in fact, that it is impossible to think about anything except the immediate sensations of sexual excitement, the deep pleasures of bodily arousal.

A similar automatic response is the process of laughter. If we think too much about why we are laughing, we find ourselves unable to continue. Edgar Allan Poe (1845) described such moments very clearly: "To indulge for a moment, in any attempt at *thought*, is to be inevitably lost, for reflection but urges us to forbear" (p. 286).

And this is why sex and humor seem such peculiar bedfellows, because, as scholars of humor have often explained, to see something as funny, we really need to separate ourselves from it and look at it from a distance, from a different perspective. Yet the truth is, sex *is* funny. It's funny before, and it's funny afterward, and it can often be pretty funny when other people are doing it. It's just not funny when *we* do it. Indeed, not only is there an ancient tradition of dirty jokes, but a long history of naughty postcards, racy comedies, cartoons, puns, and skits that all operate on the premise that sex is not just funny, it's downright thigh-slappingly hilarious. Watch any current sit-com, read any magazine, look at the greeting card rack in your local stationery store—we are constantly surrounded by not-so-subtle double entendres that make our human need for sex into one enormous joke.

Cognitive joke theorists argue that all a joke's humor is in what Freud (1905) called the "joke work." In most "dirty" jokes, this clearly involves the release of sexual repression, both individual and cultural. Legman believes that our constant need to laugh about sex is a result of our anxiety about it—our recognition that sex, when it comes down to it, is highly peculiar and undignified. He asserts that erotic humor is so popular mainly because there is so much anxiety in human society about the sexual impulse, and dirty jokes are ubiquitous because their real point is to shake off the unease and insecurity we feel about the innate absurdity of the sexual act. In other words, the enormous amount of humor that surrounds the subject of sex is symptomatic of the unconscious fear and anxiety provoked by any manifestation, however lighthearted, of the human body distorted, truncated, *out of control*, and thereby made abject and exliminal. The indignity of the human body engaged in the sexual act mimics a leveling, a dissolution of hierarchies, a collapse of values. A horror of undifferentiated, disorganized, uncontrolled relations is echoed in the laughter inspired by the sexual act—a vision of human bodies that are mutilated, interwoven, crossed over, etiolated, doubled, or incomplete.

According to anthropologist Mary Douglas (1978), the laughter provoked by jokes is a form of *antirite:*

The rite imposes order and harmony, while the joke disorganizes. From the physical, to the personal, to the social, to the cosmic, great rituals claim unity in experience. They assert hierarchy and order. In doing so, they affirm the value of the symbolic patterning of the universe. Each level of patterning is validated and enriched by association with the rest. But jokes have the opposite effect. They do not affirm the dominant values, but denigrate and devalue [p. 102].

During the 1950s, many psychoanalysts still agreed with the basic premise behind Freud's writings on jokes, and many undertook experiments similar in nature to Legman's. For example, psychoanalyst Silvano Arieti (1950) examined the relationship between different kinds of wit and humor and specific psychological and neurological disorders. And Redlich, Levine, and Sohler (1951) developed a psychodiagnostic technique in which the patient selected his or her likes and dislikes from different examples of cartoons. Significantly, a number of psychotherapists during the 1950s found therapeutic benefits in requesting that a client report a favorite joke.

For example, possibly influenced by Legman's (1951) piece on the dirty joke, as early as 1955 psychoanalyst Israel Zwerling was recommending the use of a patient's favorite joke as a diagnostic aid. While admitting that this procedure did not necessarily afford him information unavailable by other means, Zwerling suggested that the joke is a metaphor for the joke teller. As with the dream, argued Zwerling, the protagonist in the joke is the one with whom the joke teller identifies, and all other characters in the joke stand for both the different selves of the teller and the important people in his or her world. Contextual and content factors are also significant, added Zwerling. He considered the situation, the stresses and emotions, and the events that take place in the joke all to be symbolic statements and hypotheses about the joke teller's lifestyle and current crises.

While Legman sticks to the analysis of what are commonly known as "dirty" jokes, he constantly makes it clear that his theories also apply to other kinds of jokes, too. More contemporary scholars of humor have taken Legman's work in interesting directions. Psychoanalyst Joseph Richman (1996), for example, regards jokes that testify to a struggle between the superego (or conscience) and the id (or self-indulgence) as the domain of obsessive-compulsive personalities; jokes often conceal psychopathic fantasies. Jokes concerning love relationships, especially jokes with erotic, oedipal or incestuous themes, are the hallmark, according to Richman, of emotionally centered or hysterical personalities. Paranoid people tell jokes in which the protagonist is victimized; manic-depressive types tell jokes featuring up-and-down imagery; and psychopaths tell jokes about flight as well as self-justification. More obviously, the slow-witted tell jokes about mental deficiency, and alcoholics tell jokes about drinking (pp. 340–345).

Jokes with violent themes, according to Richman, are sometimes told as a warning of self-destructive tendencies in the teller. Richman and Mango (1990) give an example of a joke told in group therapy by "Chaz," a chronically depressed alcoholic patient:

Kids were playing in the schoolyard and a fight broke out.
"What happened?" asked the teacher.
"Someone got hit in the ass," said the kid.
"You mean rectum," the teacher replied.
"Not rectum," said the kid. "It really killed him."

The death theme in that joke is ominous; this patient committed suicide two months later. "In retrospect," write Richman and Mango, "we could see his jokes . . . as cries for help" (p. 118).

Although Legman's work began to be taken more seriously during the 1950s and 60s, he continued to separate himself from the cultural establishment. "Let us not be taken in by the 'literachoor' background of my writing: I am a social and pop-culch critic," he wrote to publisher Nathaniel Tarn in 1967. "I do not give a damn for literature, and consider it to be entirely without audience, today, except for college professors looking to Publish and not Perish" (Legman to Nathaniel Tarn, December 15, 1967, Nathaniel Tarn Papers). With statements like these, Legman consciously estranged himself from any form of academic life.

Despite his antiacademic inclinations, however, Legman's arguments are sustained by an informed understanding of psychoanalytic theory and by a prodigious knowledge of the classics. His intellectual grounding is Freudian psychoanalysis viewed through a strong lens of sexual and social idealism, and his theoretical ideas clearly belong to the Freudian (1905) orthodoxy. But Legman takes Freud's ideas one step further by obliterating the distinction Freud made between the abstract (or innocent) and the tendentious (or hostile) joke. To Legman, all dirty jokes are essentially hostile in nature.

Like the rest of Legman's work, the *Rationale* boils over with learned allusions, psychoanalytic evaluations, value judgments, and irrational attacks. In the space of a single page, he might dabble in philosophy, attack medicine, engage in literary critique, and offer a personal anecdote about his intimate relationships with women. His prose is always full of liberating verve, color, and exhaustively documented diatribes, relieved from time to time by wonderfully slanderous attacks on famous people and an obsession with scarcely relevant minutiae. At one point, for example —and apropos of nothing in particular—he launches on a rant against "the neurotic modern regression to the anal stage," which, he claims, is behind the contemporary interest in deodorants:

> The natural odors of the woman are to be washed away as "dirt," and are to be replaced by the anal and genital secretions of deer (musk), skunks (civet), beavers (castor), and diseased whales (ambergris) at $30 an ounce. The natural secretions of the woman are free. . . . In the battle between the neurotic modern regression to the anal stage, expressed with the reaction-formation minus sign of an excessive interest in "cleanliness," white bathroom, and even kitchen fixtures, mentholated toilet paper, special "body-odor" soaps and "chlorophyll" *ex votos* that make the human being (and bathroom) smell like a freshly creosoted chicken-coop, a few desperate avowals of wholesome interest in the natural body (though seldom in its natural odors) can sometimes still be found [Legman, 1968, p. 454].

Rationale of the Dirty Joke was reviewed seriously, though not always positively, in a number of academic journals. Richard E. Buehler (1970) praised it as "extremely readable, enjoyable, and challenging," yet, in the next sentence, he described its author as "wrongheaded and subjective" (p. 87). Buehler's review was substantial and serious, but he found a good deal in the book to dislike. Far more positive was an anonymous (1971) article in the *Psychoanalytic Review* that gave the book wholesale approval, a response that must have been very satisfying to the self-educated Legman. The reviewer described the *Rationale* as

a very erudite psychological, sociological, cultural and psycho-analytic treatise on how various types of human sexual behaviours are seen and evaluated in terms of humor . . . [while] the book does not tell us whether Mr. Legman has been in analysis, [its author displays] a very knowledgeable grasp of psychoanalytic concepts [p. 644].

Outside the academic world, however, reviewers were far less kind. Three major reviews of the book were published in the mainstream press—one (a review of the American edition) in the *New York Review of Books* on April 10, 1969, and two (of the British edition) in the *Listener* on September 11, 1969, and in the *New Statesman* on August 29, 1969.

British object relations psychoanalyst Charles Rycroft (1969) described the *Rationale* as "difficult to take seriously" for a variety of reasons. First, he complained, Legman's categorization of jokes according to their subject matter did not take into account that jokes are mainly an oral phenomenon, told by particular people in particular situations, whose meaning often depends on the context in which they are told. Second, he argued, classifying jokes according to their overt subject matter does not make much sense if, as Legman is claiming, most of these jokes seem to have meanings that are implicit, proverbial, or metaphorical in nature. "This arrangement," argued Rycroft, "is as confusing as a book on proverbs would be if it insisted on discussing sayings about too many cooks spoiling the broth and people having their cake and eating it as though they were about cooking" (pp. 24–25).

Third, like many other readers, Rycroft found Legman's eccentric style and intemperate language so difficult to put up with that it caused him to "lose all faith" in the author's judgment:

> Among his hates are D. H. Lawrence ("a physical weakling dreaming of rape"), Ernest Hemingway, Graham Greene, Marshall McLuhan, Arthur Machen ("a half-baked exotic"), digit-dialing, zip codes, hippies, science fiction, women who swear, smoke, drink or shave their armpits, doctors, psychiatrists, and most (but not all) writers of sex manuals. Even Freud is not spared a snide crack or two, notwithstanding Legman's total but non-comprehending intellectual dependence on him [pp. 24–25].

The last point is made much of. Rycroft believed Legman's knowledge of Freudian psychoanalysis to be simplified and inadequate; he argued that many of Legman's interpretations seem broadly drawn and unsophisticated. He claimed that Legman seemed unaware of the more subtle work Freud did after the 1920s, and "is totally ignorant of the developments [in psychoanalysis] of the last fifty years" (pp. 24–25).

Philip French (1969) was a little more sympathetic, pointing out that "Legman has a lot of weird and wonderful learning to vouchsafe to us" (p. 278). In general, however, his review was also negative; like Rycroft, French drew attention to Legman's precarious system of classification and suggested that this kind of vague theme-indexing lay itself open to duplication—a criticism that is often made about Legman's work ("to read it once is to read it twice," is how French put it [p. 279]). French also complained that a slight change of emphasis or approach could easily lead to the same joke's appearing in a number of different sections. "Moreover [Legman] is infinitely repetitive; indeed, one gets the impression in reading the book from cover to cover that one is doing something the author hasn't done" (p. 279).

Most scathing of all, however, was the review by Brigid Brophy (1969), which accused Legman of inaccuracy, illiteracy, bad grammar, arrogance, ignorance of English phonetics, perverse judgments, misogyny, and a host of other failings. Brophy especially criticized the fact that Legman never discusses the connection between dirty jokes and set-piece jokes in general and never considers what it is that makes a dirty joke "dirty." Like Rycroft and French, she also objected to Legman's overheated prose style and accused him of "purple-faced passages of belly-laughable rationale" (p. 350). She added that "anyone determined to get a laugh out of his book would do best to seek it not in the stories, but in the commentary" (p. 351). She found Legman's attitude toward women ridiculously anachronistic but was mostly offended by his paranoid rants against homosexuals:

> For Mr. Legman, "homosexuality" is regularly a term of abuse—and an implicit malapropism, since his practice shows he thinks it applies only to men. Exactly what he thinks wrong with homosexuality he never says . . . Mr. Legman believes in a (male) homosexual conspiracy: "the 'camp' commissioners of the Homosexual Internationale and the sick female fag-hags who help publicize them." . . . And he warns women that fashion in clothes is imposed on them "by homosexuals who hate them" [p. 350].

While the subject of his work and the nature of his writing style made Legman something of an easy target for ridicule, many of the points of criticism raised in those three reviews are valid, some more than others. It may be true that Legman often wanders from his subject matter; but what these reviewers seem to have missed is that the goal of his scholarship is to understand how and why everything links and locks together, including especially mimetic representations or articulations and physical acts. The objective of Legman's work is essentially the reintegration and assimilation of apparently disparate elements, so they can be seen as existing along a complex political, social, and psychological continuum—as Bruce Jackson (1977) puts it, "a world where *everything counts*" (p. 112).

Moreover, all three reviewers seem to have been taken aback by the fact that, throughout the book, its author constantly offers evaluations of behavior and situations and frequently makes value judgments, which "serious" scholars apparently should not do. "This is unfashionable now," wrote Legman to author Christine Nasso (1977), "but is the only responsible position" (p. 526). It is also true that Legman sometimes exaggerates the facts and makes outrageous claims, but he does so only as a rhetorical device to draw attention to some particular circumstance or situation; his hyperbole is usually proof of his earnestness.

Significantly, the title of Legman's (1968) book, *Rationale of the Dirty Joke*, was very consciously and deliberately chosen, and this is something else that all its reviewers seem to have misunderstood. All three reviewers seem to have assumed that the point of the book was to *explain* the dirty joke, which as Rycroft rightly suggests, would involve a psychological study of both teller and listener, of the context in which the joke is being told, and a performative analysis taking into account all aspects of the joke-telling dynamic.

But Legman is attempting something rather more subtle; he is trying to understand what the dirty joke *itself* is striving to explain—to understand the rules of the world *within* the joke. In other words, he wants to explain how the dirty joke makes rational something apparently nonrational. In his introduction, Legman carefully explains that the title of the *Rationale* indicates that the book is an attempt to understand how "these stories and individuals do personify what the tellers and singers well know to be real but inexplicable peculiarities of human behavior, which they are attempting somehow to fit into a rational view of the world, whether as horror or as humor" (p. 22). None of the reviewers of the *Rationale* seem to have understood this, though Legman goes to great lengths to make it explicit.

Nor do any of the reviews credit the enormous amount of work involved in simply collecting and categorizing 30 years' worth of dirty jokes, work entailing, as Legman explains, daily struggles "under the gross tonnage of 60,000 index cards and some 10,000 books" (p. 14). However fruitless this work may have seemed to those reviewing the *Rationale*, it has proved enormously valuable to folklore scholars and lexicographers and was completed in the face of a deep-seated contempt from established academics and under a set of financial strictures that most scholars and writers would have found completely disabling.

The second volume of *Rationale of the Dirty Joke*, *No Laughing Matter* (Legman, 1975), contains the dirtiest jokes of all, what Legman sometimes refers to as the "nasty-nasties." Categories include Homosexuality,

Prostitution, Disease and Disgust, Castration, Dysphemism and Insults, and Scatology; subcategories include Defecation, Feces as Gift, Anal Sadism, and Semen as Food. "This book," warns its author, "is full of material so disgusting that it will make any decent, clean, healthy person want to throw up" (p. 14).

In the introduction to *No Laughing Matter*, Legman repeats his argument that the same dirty jokes are told everywhere and have been told throughout history, though in mutated forms that reflect the particular characteristics of the countries they pass through. He also repeats his belief that dirty jokes create an arsenal or form of defense to turn away attackers; "under the mask of humor," he writes, "all men are enemies" (p. 10). In this context, he refers to an important passage in Freud on the compulsive and often hysterical telling of anti-Jewish jokes—the tellers themselves being Jewish—during the dangerous anti-Semitic period of the Dreyfus trial just preceding World War I in Europe (Legman also always disliked Woody Allen movies, which he regarded as vehicles for unappetizing anti-Jewish humor).[3] These are classic examples, according to Legman, of the joke as a form of confessional—the teller's desperate begging for forgiveness, or *shriving*. He explains this complex with characteristic heated eloquence:

> The cycle of telling and listening, listening and telling must be endlessly and compulsively repeated for a lifetime, the teller visibly taking the least pleasure of all in the humor at which he struggles so hard, and in which, at the end, he stands like the hungry child he is, darkly famished at their feasting while the audience laughs [p. 47].

Legman also points out that his own name is essentially a kind of dirty joke—he happens to have been a "tit-man" rather than a "leg-man"—

---

[3] There is a substantial literature on the anxious and neurotic aspects of Jewish humor. Ted Cohen (1999) argues that Jewish humor is quintessentially the humor of the outsider; Peter Kivy (2003) makes the point that Jewish joking is notoriously clannish and, because of the nature of the Jewish clan, is intensely outer directed in an especially aggressive way (p. 13).

which may have kicked off his whole interest in the phenomenon of the dirty joke in the first place (p. 14). Later he discusses the magical significance of other people's names, a significance he believes to be connected to the notion that what one says can have a physical effect on the person one says it to (a notion that survives in the current libel laws). Legman argues that this is the modern counterpart of the ancient idea of the evil eye (p. 241),[4] a superstition that still reveals itself in the apotropaic value of belittling one's own possessions ("the idea that the 'evil eye' can be averted by saying 'Oh, *that* old thing!' when some article or achievement is complimented" [p. 302]).

No Laughing Matter is not just a book about dirty jokes, but a book about *really* dirty jokes. While acknowledging that almost all humor is composed of an "inevitable and hostile infantile anality" (p. 891), Legman warns us that the jokes in this volume are more hostile and more anal than most. He then proceeds to run through a litany of stories about fecal matter, necrophilia, venereal disease, urine, and sputum. He describes their regular style of delivery, in which the most repulsive details are frequently repeated again and again, as if to bring the listener "as close as possible to vomiting" (p. 382). Obviously, states Legman, there is nothing very "funny" about such jokes.

So why do people tell them? According to Legman, the prevailing emotion behind such jokes is *fear*—in particular, fear of being driven away and denied (he points out that the "*casting off of fear* by rollicking in its details is the one classic function of jokes and humor generally" [p. 302]). This function applies especially to stories about unusual sexual practices, like necrophilia, for example, or "fart-smelling," scatology, and undinism (especially jokes about women pissing in men's beards and faces). The teller of such jokes, explains Legman,

> is not really at ease in the slime and blood and pus with which he often splatters his stories for cake-topping, in the disfigurements and castrations he habitually uses for décor, his face more

---

[4] Legman (1975) draws our attention to Seligman's (1910) *Der Böse Blick*, which Legman describes as "the standard source on the subject."

often than not contorted into a fixed grin as he crashes on: a grin representing his nervous and guilty enjoyment of his listeners' unease. From any point of view, the scene is like the definition of a German joke: "*No laughing matter*" [p. 32].

One of the longest and most controversial sections of the second volume deals with jokes on the topic of Legman's favorite bugbear, homosexuality. As in the first volume, his attitude is aggressively antihomosexual. In introducing one story, for example, he explains that its intention is to mock the British, "*all* of whom are considered practically homosexual at a certain level in American folklore. (This is not altogether folklore)" (p. 93). The following two examples of homosexual jokes may shed some light on Legman's virulent antihomosexual feelings. Both jokes are taken from the category of "Pedication," and both have the same punchline, though used to a very different effect in each case:

Two sailors are talking aboard ship.
"You know," says one, "The best tail I've ever had was right here on this ship."
"No shit?"
"Well, not really enough to matter."

According to Legman, jokes like this one disguise homosexual fears and inclinations. This particular joke touches, "lightly but certainly," on "the one most inacceptable element in pedication: the dirtying of the active male's penis with feces. This does not always happen, but once is enough. This is also why cultivated men will not perform pedication with women" (p. 151). Legman also believes that the purely linguistic approach to the homosexual act of sodomy functions as a sort of "linguistic tongs," which can then be "used by the joke-tellers to deal antiseptically with a subject obviously of great interest to them, yet from which they must pointedly withdraw insofar as any 'personal' interest is concerned" (p. 147). It is for this reason, explains Legman, that many people will tell homosexual jokes "with exaggerated homosexual intonation and gestures, though the same persons will often not bother to attempt dialect effects in telling, for example, comedy Jewish, Negro or Italian stories" (p. 147).

The second joke goes like this:

A cowpuncher rode in off the range on a charcoal gray horse, with a pink dotted-Swiss saddle, and tied its satin reins to the hitching rail at the saloon. Then he pranced inside, adjusted his lavender chaps, and said in a high, mincing voice, "Where'th the fellowth?"
The bartender said, "They're out at Boot Hill, hanging a queer."
So the cowboy boomed in a deep voice, "NO SHIT?"

This joke is included in a category that Legman calls "The Tough Faggot." Such jokes, he argues,

neatly unveil what is perhaps the commonest of all homosexual disguises: that of super-toughness—the cowboy, the truck-driver, the athlete, the prize-fighter and bullfighter, the explorer and animal-killer, and the professional soldier; all of those professions which turn out, on closer study, to be the rendezvous largely of homosexual sadistic types in flight from any public recognition of their essentially sexual neurosis [p. 82].

While *No Laughing Matter* was reviewed positively in the *Journal of American Folklore* (Boehler, 1970), these kinds of arch-Freudian "diagnoses" turned many readers off the book, and others found it difficult to take the second volume seriously. For example, R. Z. Sheppard (1975) described Legman as "the Joe McCarthy of heterosexuality, who looks for gays under every bed" (p. 97). He also accused Legman of harboring an idealistic, Victorian view of the purity and transcendence of womanhood, of being the kind of man who believes his wife should be kept at home, barefoot and pregnant.[5] Nevertheless, Sheppard's review was one of the most positive Legman's work ever received, and ends on a high note:

---

[5] Some of Legman's early work was published under the name Gershon Legman Keith, after his first wife, Beverley Keith. It is difficult to understand why a man with his views would take his wife's name, something Legman elected to do when he was first married. Sheppard was obviously not aware of this fact.

Rationale of the Dirty Joke is an undeniable presence, a work of majestic ego that was weathered by new attitudes and ideas long before completion. In the future, it will be plundered, measured, and thumbed through for titillation. But the book will remain impervious in all its pocked dignity, authenticity and embattled romanticism [p. 96].

In fact, Legman was reportedly so pleased with this last sentence that, even into his eighth decade, he considered it to be the perfect epitaph for his life and work.

CHAPTER 3

Against Laughter

In *Rationale of the Dirty Joke*, Legman (1968) claims that the inspiration behind his life's work on jokes originally came from Victor Hugo's 1869 novel, *The Man Who Laughs*. The hero of this story, Gwynplaine, is stolen as an infant by a band of *comprachicos*, child-farmers who distort the features and stunt the growth of children so they make more effective beggars. Gwynplaine's mouth is carved by the *comprachicos* into a terrible permanent rictus that causes "implacable hilarity" wherever he goes:

> Intense anxiety, disappointment, disgust and chagrin were all depicted in the rigid features; but a ghastly smile wreathed the lips, imparting an expression of lugubrious mirth to the entire countenance. . . . Those who eagerly crowded around to gaze at this grim exemplification of the covert sarcasm and irony which dwells in every human breast, nearly died with laughter at the sepulchral immobility of the sneering smile [p. 298].

As "The Laughing Man," Gwynplaine becomes a successful mountebank. Since no one can see him without laughing, he makes a living by exhibiting himself in a traveling show and quickly becomes all the rage. "The listless came to laugh, the melancholy came to laugh, evil consciences came to laugh—a laugh so irresistible that it seemed almost an epidemic," writes Hugo (p. 333), and yet once the laughter is over, Gwynplaine is "impossible to contemplate" (p. 299).

The Man Who Laughs is perhaps one of the most vivid and profound studies of human laughter ever written. Hugo, particularly adept at describing the function of laughter in social and crowd situations, points out that "a laugh is often a refusal" (p. 22) and that "men's laughter sometimes exerts all its power to murder" (p. 205). The story poignantly depicts the way in which "the grotesque is linked with the sublime . . . the laugh echoes the groan, parody rides behind despair" (p. 311). Gwynplaine's distorted face immediately produces the effect of violent laughter, which, for Hugo, provokes the central question of the novel: "Is laughter a synonym for joy?" (p. 295).

This is the question at the heart of both the *Rationale of the Dirty Joke* and *No Laughing Matter*. In these two gargantuan works, Legman extends his argument about laughter as a response to jokes to apply to human laughter in general, which he regards as a repressed and evasive response to anxiety and neurosis. Legman's sensitivity to the psychodynamics of laughter is consistently fascinating. In *No Laughing Matter* (1975), he describes, in eloquent if hyperbolic terms, the different varieties of human laughter, including "yoiks of wild humor" (p. 155) and nervous or so-called polite Japanese laughter: "the inane tittering and fishlike sucking-in of the breath of everyone in Japan from geisha girls on up to top-hatted diplomats at moments of conventional falsity and difficulty" (p. 9). He also describes the grin of the joke teller that "can sometimes escalate itself into perfectly hysterical laughter, with the teller falling on the wall or floor, and being completely unable to go on" (p. 22). Similarly, psychoanalyst Martin Grotjahn (1957) describes the "belly laugh" as standing halfway between the socially accepted noise of laughter and certain toilet noises that are taboo in company (p. 75). And Legman (1975) reminds us of the listener who breaks up uncontrollably in convulsive laughter "to the point of becoming physically weak, farting loudly, or literally 'pissing in their pants'—women especially, as to this last" (p. 812).[1]

Laughter is also infectious. In a way, it has its effect only on those

---

[1] Judith Legman recalls a female friend of her husband's who always described comic movies as falling into the category of a "one pantser" or a "two pantser," depending on how much they made her laugh.

who believe in it. As Legman explains, like the dybbuk, wandering soul or "outhouse demon" of Jewish mythology, laughter enters unwanted into the body of the person thus "possessed," who can rid himself or herself of this undesirable gift only by passing it on to another, like a hex. He also points out that the taboos surrounding human laughter are similar to those concerning other physiological motor impulses, such as sneezing, vomiting, and ejaculation, and are surrounded by similarly enormous structures of social gesture. Unlike many similar bodily impulses, however, laughter is seldom associated with a sense of revulsion or religious taboo.

My aim in this chapter is to use the work of Legman to suggest that human laughter is perhaps as much about neurosis as catharsis and to remind us of Nietzsche's (1901) claim that "man alone suffers so excruciatingly in the world that he was compelled to invent laughter" (p. 18).

Throughout history, a number of perceptive writers and artists have displayed an intuitive, almost instinctive grasp of the fundamentally neurotic nature of some kinds of human laughter. For example, in *Death in Venice,* Thomas Mann (1912) describes how his protagonist, Gustav von Aschenbach, sitting in his chair on the hotel terrace, bears witness to the terrifying presence of a traveling minstrel: "the Neapolitan comic type, half pimp, half actor, brutal and bold-faced, dangerous and entertaining" (p. 249). Aschenbach finds the troubadour "indecent" and "offensive" and is particularly disturbed by "his grimaces and bodily movements," and "his way of winking suggestively and lasciviously licking the corner of his mouth" (p. 249). Significantly, the singer smells strongly of the carbolic antiseptic being used to disinfect the city and conceal the deathly stench of the plague that has been borne in on the sirocco and to which Aschenbach has already, albeit unknowingly, fallen victim. The minstrel's performance is terrifying because it consists of nothing but hollow, raucous laughter:

It was a song that Aschenbach could not remember ever having heard before; a bold hit in an unintelligible dialect, and having a laughing refrain . . . a burst of laughter, to some extent rhythmically ordered but treated with a high degree of naturalism, the soloist in particular showing great talent in his lifelike rendering of it. With artistic distance restored between himself and the spectators, he had recovered all his impudence, and the simulated laughter which he shamelessly directed at the terrace was a laughter of mockery. . . . He would pretend to be struggling with an irresistible impulse of hilarity. He would sob, his voice would waver, he would press his hand against his mouth and hunch his shoulders, till . . . the laughter would burst out of him, exploding in a wild howl, with such authenticity that it was infectious and communicated itself to the audience, so that a wave of objectless and merely self-propagating merriment swept over the terrace as well. . . . He bent his knees, slapped his thighs, held his sides, he nearly burst with what was no longer laughing but shrieking; he pointed his finger up at the guests, as if that laughing company above him were itself the most comical thing in the world, and in the end they were all laughing, everyone in the garden and on the verandah, the waiters and the lift boys and the house servants in the doorways. . . . Aschenbach reclined in his chair no longer, he was sitting bolt upright as if trying to fend off an attack or flee from it [p. 251].

But he is, of course, unable to escape, since the combination of the minstrel's abominable laughter and the hospital smell of the carbolic hold him in an "immobilizing nightmare," an "unbreakable and inescapable spell that held his mind and senses captive" (p. 251).

This evil trickster is clearly descended from the posturing fools and acrobats of the Italian *Commedia de l'Arte*, which, like most protothe-atrical forms, was a significant area of homosexual activity. In *No Laughing Matter*, Legman (1975) points out how "circus clowns and carnival enter-tainers have largely been homosexual or pre-psychotic (or both) since very remote times" (p. 935). A repellent and semicriminal outcast, the street clown is at the same time our familiar, able to charm and entertain us with his unexpected wit, sometimes even regarded as the God-touched vessel through whom the sacred powers could transmit messages, the Holy Fool of the Middle Ages about whom it was often said *nobis est et speculum* ("he is our mirror").

In Mann's (1912) *Death in Venice*, the mocking laughter of the debauched troubadour combines ridicule with sexual menace and, at least for Aschenbach, embodies the trauma of an apocalyptic revelation. The minstrel's carbolic stink reveals that the plague has finally penetrated the grounds of the hotel; it has infected its inhabitants, and his sexual scuttle and cackling impel in Aschenbach an attack of homosexual panic, heightened by the close presence of "the beautiful boy," Tadzio. In the foul stench of the troubadour, and in the decadent abandon of his laughter, Aschenbach comes face to face with the vision of his own decaying soul.

Here laughter is a form of revelation, expressive of corruption, malady, and dissolution, and closely allied with physical pathology and illness. The "infectious" laughter of the troubadour seems to provide an aural correlative for the plague that is currently sweeping Venice; his sobs, shrieks, and "wild howls" represent the virulent eruption of Aschenbach's infection. In this scene, through the assault of the minstrel's laughter, Aschenbach comes personally to grasp the reality of his artistic failure, his homosexual compulsions, his bodily decay, and his imminent death.

A similar scene of terrifying laughter takes place in Nathanael West's (1939) dark fantasy, *Day of the Locust*. Failed circus clown Harry Greener has "a variety of laughs, all of them theatrical," including "a victim's laugh"—which he practices "like a musician tuning up before a concert" (p. 70). In this scene, Harry uses his repertoire of laughter to assault his daughter, Faye:

He didn't want to laugh, but a short bark escaped before he could stop it. He waited anxiously to see what would happen. When it didn't hurt he laughed again. He kept on, timidly at first, then with growing assurance. He laughed with his eyes closed and the sweat pouring down his brow. . . . This new laugh was not critical; it was horrible. When she was a child, he used to punish her with it. It was his masterpiece. There was a director who always called on him to give it when he was shooting a scene in an insane asylum or a haunted castle. . . . It began with a sharp, metallic crackle, like burning sticks, then gradually increased in volume until it became a rapid bark, then fell away again to an obscene chuckle. After a slight pause, it climbed until it was the nicker of a horse, then still higher to become a machinelike screech. . . . Faye listened helplessly with her head on one side. Suddenly she too laughed, not willingly, but fighting the sound [pp. 76–77].

Harry's laughter is empty and apocalyptic and exposes the essential sterility of his consciousness. The revelation it brings is the rejection of every form of consoling fantasy; as an expression of *taedium vitae comicus*, it embodies the dreary pointlessness of Harry's failed life and exposes his status as a victim of absurd and spiritless illusions. In particular, it reveals the misery and loneliness at the heart of Harry's compulsive clowning and functions as a symptom of the unnamed illness that is soon to claim his life. This is sordid, petty laughter, the laughter of failure, exposing the pervasiveness of human misery and suffering, stripping us of all our traditional ideals and all the illusions we have about ourselves. In Nathanael West, as Walter Poznar (1983) puts it, "man stands as a being bereft of every consoling grace, a cipher, maudlin beyond imagining, pathetic beyond description, trapped like Sartre's dramatic protagonists in a hell from which there is no exit" (pp. 115–116).

These two fictional scenes give us a brief glimpse into the abyss of emotions that can underlie human laughter. The minstrel's laughter in *Death in Venice* is cruel, bitter, and degrading—an attempt to gain ascendancy over all that is vile in humanity by relishing it gleefully; in *Day of the Locust*, Harry Greener's laughter is full of malice, loneliness, and fear. Both scenes use laughter to evoke the specter of madness and the decay of the body; both expose the agony and suffering of the human consciousness. In these scenes, both writers use laughter to evoke a mood of violent despair.

Between 1964 and 1967, anthropologist Colin Turnbull went to live among the Ik people, a Ugandan mountain tribe whose society was disintegrating after years of drought and starvation. Turnbull's (1972) account of his life with the Ik, *The Mountain People*, chronicles a society in such a desperate state of existence that all "human" qualities—family, cooperative society, love, hope, faith—have collapsed, for, among a people dying of starvation, such qualities militate against survival. According to Turnbull's account, the degeneration of society among the Ik was so complete that mothers left their children to die, neighbors defecated on one another's doorsteps, children took food out of one another's mouths, and the stronger people vomited so as to have room in their stomachs to eat what belonged to the weak.

And yet what disturbed Turnbull most about the Ik was their laughter and "an indefinable absence of something that should have been there, perhaps in its place" (p. 112). The Ik had reverted to a state of inhumanity, of mutual hostility and aloneness characterized by the symbolic violence of laughter and derision. Laughter was the Ik's most common reaction to the horrors surrounding them; it was considered a perfectly appropriate reaction to suffering and desperation and was not condemned as particularly rude and callous. Laughter was their response to everything—the death of loved ones and family members, danger and pain, trauma and violence; and, finally, to the rape of children, to famine, starvation, and death.

For the Ik, pathological laughter was the main symptom of a mass reversal of humanity, incorporating the complete dissolution of family life, total valuelessness, apathy, and collapse. It was a manifest reaction to spiritual decay, withdrawal, depression, and suicide. According to anthropologist John Calhoun (1972), it served as an accompaniment to such rites of self-mutilation as ripping out one's own testes or chopping off one's nose (p. 316). According to Turnbull's account, the Ik howled with laughter on occasions that would normally evoke horror or great anxiety: when young children accidentally plunged their hands into the fire; when babies fell out of their slings to the ground; when family members died of starvation; when a man convicted of adultery was burned to death, and any similar occasion of others' misfortune. Bereft of love, hope, or any belief in the future, the Ik had nothing left but laughter, which quickly became the most appropriate reaction to the pain and misery surrounding them.

When all faith and friendship had died, laughter remained, expressive only of corruption, malady, and dissolution. The derisive laughter of the Ik seems to have expressed a sense of simultaneous identification and alienation, the sense that the horrors that provoked this terrifying laughter could happen to any member of the tribe, at any time. In other words, it could have been them, but this time it was not. This is a form of violent derision that, at least for a moment, makes the heart stronger. When an old man is knocked to the ground, onlookers respond with "shrieks of delighted laughter" (p. 206). When a child is fatally ill with an intestinal blockage, his father calls people over to laugh at the boy's distended belly. When people get so hungry they are able only to crawl, others laugh at the crawlers and push them "so that they teetered and then toppled" (p. 224). When a blind, elderly widow falls down a mountainside and lies at the bottom on her back, her legs and arms thrashing feebly, "a little crowd standing on the edge above looked down at her and laughed at the spectacle" (p. 226). This last incident began to convince Turnbull that laughter is perhaps the most rational reaction to so bleak and hopeless a situation, since any other response would point to the vestigial remains of those human fantasies and illusions of faith and fraternity that, among the Ik, had long ago disintegrated:

> In the end, I had a greater respect for the Ik, and I wonder if their way was not right, if I too should not have stood with the little crowd at the top of the *oror* and laughed as *Lo'ono* flopped about like a withered old tortoise on its back, then left her to die, perhaps laughing at herself, instead of crying [p. 228].

The chilling plight of the Ik may help us to understand how part of the function of laughter is to vivify the manifest incongruity between human social organization and the uncontrollable nature of the polluting human body, an understanding that, ironically, only reinforces the strictures of human culture.

A great deal has been written about the literary manifestations of perverse or evil laughter, perhaps most acutely in Maxime Prévost's (2002) *Rictus Romantiques*. Prévost considers the role of satanic laughter (*le rire de force*) in melodrama and the gothic novel, the perverse laughter uttered by Frankenstein's monster, Charles Maturin's (1821) Melmoth, and Polidori's Vampire. Less attention has been paid, however, to the aesthetic and philosophical implications of this kind of laughter when it is manifested in psychiatric patients, in which it is generally referred to as "pathological laughter" and usually occurs in connection with certain diseases of the central nervous system.

Medical cases are often reported for which laughter is not a *cure* for the disease, but a *symptom* of it. Psychiatric studies of patients suffering from pathological laughter suggest that mirth (the subjective feeling of merriment or amusement) and laughter (the facial respiratory and other related motor acts associated with mirth) are separate functions that can be neurologically disassociated (see, e.g., Arlazaroff et al., 1998). In fact, studies by McGhee (1983) and LaFrance (1983) suggest that laughter is only mildly correlated with the experience of humor, more strongly among women and less strongly among men.

Pathological laughter, usually associated with paroxysmal alterations and epileptiform manifestations, is often linked to congenital syndromes, neurological damage, acquired diseases, or metabolic defects. Uncontrollable attacks of mirthless laughter often precede the onset of apoplectic attacks and are also sometimes experienced after front temporal lobe stroke and subdural hematoma. Pathological laughter is sometimes a condition of sclerosis and can often accompany certain forms of neuralgia (see, e.g., Shafquat et al., 1998). This kind of laughter takes a variety of forms, including *enuresis risoria*, or "giggle incontinence," the *fou rire prodomique* (a sudden display of mad laughter), and the *risus sardonicus*, or "devil's smile."[2]

The psychiatric literature contains some interesting examples of pathological laughter. Arlazaroff et al. (1998) describe the case of a 61-year-old woman who presented a six-month history of abrupt and continuous spells of loud, inappropriate laughter not associated with joy or humor. While speaking, she would burst into sudden loud and monotonous laughter lasting for several minutes, stopping as abruptly as she started, devoid of

---

[2] It should be noted that, according to Mendez, Nakawatase, and Brown (1999), "[D]isorders of laughter are distinct from disorders of mirth or humor, such as *moria* or *witzelsucht*. *Moria* (foolish or silly euphoria) and *witzelsucht* (a tendency to inappropriate jokes) occur with frontal lobe disorders such as neurosyphilis . . . Patients with these disorders have a habitual routine of jokes and witticisms, but they are paradoxically insensitive to humor" (p. 254).

emotional expression and with "an atmosphere of emptiness" (p. 185). The same article describes the case of a 65-year-old male who would suddenly and unexpectedly grin and would then proceed with a long spell of laughter, during which his facial expression was "devoid of mirth" (p. 185). Both patients were found to be suffering from neurological abnormalities.

Most disturbing of all is a case study reported by psychiatrists Mendez, Nakawatase, and Brown (1999) of a 67-year-old man who suffered from involuntary and unremitting laughter for *20 years*. After a series of complicated neurological procedures, the patient suffered from continuous involuntary laughter and inappropriate hilarity:

> To the utter annoyance of family and friends, the patient spent most of the day laughing, even when he felt sad. His laughter intruded in all of his conversations and was triggered by the most trivial and inconsequential stimuli. Only sleep provided respite from laughing. In recent months, his laughter had become even more disturbing to his family. Furthermore, because of his inability to stop laughing, the patient had not been able to work [p. 254].

As Victor Hugo (1869) comments of Gwynplaine, "What a weight for the shoulders of a man—an everlasting laugh!" (p. 298).

Many other cases have been reported in which no neurological damage was present and the only manifestation of illness was outbursts of inappropriate laughter. One case, reported by Arlazaroff et al. (1998), concerned a 42-year-old woman who suffered from spells of inappropriate and uncontrollable laughter almost every day, sometimes more than once a day. Her laughter was accompanied not by a sense of joy or any other pleasurable feeling, but rather by distress and anxiety. These laughing spells occurred "mainly in stressful or delicate situations, e.g., during marital disputes and on a visit to bereaved friends, causing extreme embarrassment" (p. 186).

Another case, reported by Shaibani, Sabbagh, and Doody (1994), describes an epidemic of involuntary laughter in East Africa, which started in a convent school and affected at least 1,000 girls and then spread to 14 other schools, forcing them to close. When the laughing girls were sent home, their mothers and other female relatives also became affected. In the end, "the epidemic spread to neighboring villages. Some patients required hospitalization from exhaustion. No organic process could explain this process. Eventually, it was attributed to 'repression'" (p. 248).

There are a number of similar psychiatric studies on the physiology of laughter, most of which deal with pathological laughter in brain and mental diseases. The psychoanalytic literature on laughter, however, is surprisingly scant. Important early works are those by Greig (1923), Gregory (1924), Kris (1940), and Grotjahn (1957), but no major works on the subject have been published in the last 50 years. Virtually all the psychoanalytic literature on laughter is classical in its theoretical orientation, with the exception of a few more recent articles, notably those by Marcos (1974), Poland (1990), and Feiner (1995).

Very few contemporary psychoanalysts have attempted to make sense of the difficult and complex relationship between "normal" and pathological laughter, perhaps because the subject is too disturbing and disorienting to make it an appealing topic of study. Moreover, instances of pathological laughter tend to be regarded as a symptom of physiological (rather than psychological) dysfunction; according to Karl Pfeifer (1994), "geniune" pathological laughter, unlike "nervous" or "social" laughter, is not causally mediated by sensations, perceptions, memories, cogitations, or other mental or psychological states (p. 157). As Oliver Sacks (1997) explains, unlike "nervous" or "social" laughter, pathological laughter tends to be "flat, expressionless, monotonous" and "mechanical" (p. 189), appears disturbing and unpleasant to those patients who suffer from it, and usually demands medical intervention.

However, as Turnbull's (1972) analysis of the Ik society makes clear, laughter without neurological damage can occur in the absence of humor, or even of pleasure. Philosopher James Sully (1902) drew attention to the fact that outbursts of laughter often follow a shock of fear. He also gave examples of nervous and embarrassed laughter; laughter as a result of feelings of "apprehensiveness, constraint and insecurity"; and "the tendency to laugh upon solemn occasions" (p. 78), especially during funerals, or upon receiving painful, shocking, or horrifying news, such as news of the death of a loved one (p. 78).

Most of us are familiar with the phenomenon of laughter as a reaction to sudden physical pain, as well as with dry, acerbic, hollow, bitter, and mocking laughter. The lack of a sustained and coherent relationship between laughter and feelings of "mirth" has been well testified. One study, conducted by Thorson and Powell (1991), reported that survivors of the San Francisco earthquake laughed at the slightest provocation; reporting on a similar study, the same scientists observed that soldiers on the verge of going into battle laugh at almost any cue (p. 69).

My point here is not that all laughter is pathological—of course, there is such a thing as appropriate, healthy, "normal" laughter. But I think that many scholars of the subject have tended to underestimate the extent to which laughter is experienced as an index of many different emotions, including anxiety, nervousness, discomfort, and even sexual arousal. In *Rationale of the Dirty Joke*, Legman (1968) draws our attention to a curious convention reported in jokes that involves the woman's *laughing* during foreplay, her nervous anxiety or sexual excitement being converted into laughter[3]: "A young man and girl are petting in the movies. The girl keeps squealing with laughter. Manager: 'What's the matter, young lady? Are you feeling hysterical?' Girl: 'No, he's feeling mine'." Or, in the form of a simple pun: "Girl to the boy who's petting her: 'Oh, I feel so silly.' Boy: 'Well, reach in here and you'll feel nuts'" (p. 402).

No medical studies (to my knowledge) have reported cases of people who have literally "died laughing," but such a phenomenon is hardly unknown. Most deaths from laughter, however, are actually caused by a side effect of that laughter—asphyxiation, for example, or cardiac arrest. In Lord Dunsany's (1916) malicious short story "The Three Infernal Jokes," 22 men die of laughter after hearing a devilish joke at a dinner party. And yet the actual cause of their deaths is not the laughter, but its by-products: one man accidentally inhales his cigar smoke; others burst blood vessels; some choke; and others succumb to nausea or heart failure.

Perhaps the most potent example of "death by laughter" is to be found in the 2000 French film *Laughter and Punishment*, director Isabelle Doval's fanciful reworking of Dostoyevsky. In this film, José Garcia plays Vincent,

---

[3] Mrs. Legman recalls having a roommate who did exactly this and had a special, high-pitched laugh for such occasions.

a popular young osteopath whose wife leaves him because of his constant need to make people laugh. Left alone, forced to confront the false mask of his public self, Vincent falls into a series of troubling fantasies in which his jokes are literally so funny they kill, inducing cardiac arrest in their accidental victims.

Those two narratives both seem to pose the same troubling question: What part of the laughter is the "laugh," and what are its side effects? In other words, how can we tell the laugher from the laugh?

French philosopher Henri Bergson (1911) asserted that laughing is "social ragging" (p. 16). According to Bergson, laughter "always implies a secret or unconscious . . . unavowed intention to humiliate and consequently to correct our neighbour, if not in his will, at least in his deed" (p. 16). In other words, when one of the human herd notices a reduction in the versatility and flexibility in one of its members, it goes through a loud series of respiratory convulsions as a way of admonishing the offending party. For Bergson, the social significance of human laughter is always inextricably associated with its aggressive intent. The laugh, according to Bergson, "always implies a secret or unconscious intent, if not against each one of us, against all events of society as a whole" (p. 18). Bergson and Freud both agreed that laughter has an aggressive function, although Bergson, afraid of finding some elements of laughter that are unflattering to humanity, was reluctant to investigate the point too closely. Moreover, despite their often conflicting views on the subject, both Freud and Bergson agreed that humor resembles mental disturbance in that a distressful or offensive idea leads to logical peculiarities.

Freud (1905) explained how unconscious material is held in repression by specific amounts of psychic energy; when some experience or observation hits on this material, the psychic energy diverted to the task of holding the material in repression becomes superfluous for a second and is thereby transformed into laughter. The importance of this theory is its understanding of laughter as an internally directed rather than externally directed process, by which one element of the unconscious may attack another. Freud considered the activity of laughter to be mainly a cathartic, pleasure-giving release. However, Freud (1930) later examined the very wide range of methods the human mind has constructed to evade the compulsion to suffer: "a series which begins in neurosis and culminates in madness, and which includes intoxication, self-absorption, and ecstasy" (p. 163). One of these methods, according to Freud, is laughter.

While Freud wrote mainly about *humor* rather than *laughter*, his analysis suggests that most forms of such pleasure come from the gratification of a forbidden, often aggressive desire. "Humor is not resigned, it is rebellious" (Freud, 1905, p. 24). Particularly hostile is what Freud referred to as "tendentious humor," that is, the veiled attack that satisfies an aggressive motive in the form of the socially acceptable "assault by joke." As Legman demonstrated in his work on jokes, the penalties for social aggression are diminished when that hostility is expressed through humor. Consequently, humor is often used as an acceptable social outlet for those frustrations, tensions, and aggressions which have no other means of release in a society that seeks to exercise control over the aggressive drives of its members.

The greater the amount of aggressive energy that is suddenly expressed, the louder and deeper the laughter will sound. Of course, the direct, undisguised outlet for aggression is not funny—an act of violence does not lead to laughter. The situation must stimulate an aggressive response, which is then repressed from consciousness into the unconscious. The aggressive feeling is disguised as laughter and can then be experienced harmlessly, at least, in social terms. And yet laughter is seldom harmless. Grotjahn (1972) gives the example of a married man who was stricken impotent when his new bride broke into uncontrollable peals of laughter at the sight of her young husband's erection: "Her laughter was an anxiety reaction. . . . she may require psychoanalytic help" (pp. 51–53).

According to Freud (1905), certain kinds of laughter function as a displacement for frightening emotions that have no other means of expression. This type of displacement is a common occurrence, as in the example given by Roy E. Russell (1996) of the carpenter who accidentally hits his thumb and responds with groans, profanity, and facial grimaces (p. 48). A less common form is the "expression displacement." This response is intended to conceal from consciousness the real character of the emotional state, as in the laughter of the Ik, which came to serve as a displaced expression of hopelessness and despair.

Early psychoanalytic studies of laughter, focusing powerfully on the personal functions and intentions of the one who laughs, revealed precisely how specific, if unconscious, motivations and satisfactions operate behind the screen of laughter. According to psychoanalysis, only when the motives of the one who laughs are recognized as paramount can laughter be understood at all. In this light, certain displays of human laughter can be seen to function as a somatic displacement of invective and abuse, revealing bitter and hostile despair. The display of neurotic or pathological laughter constitutes a ritual form of protective cover, a socially sanctioned disguise. To put it more simply, it isn't that we laugh "at" someone or "with" someone; it isn't that we laugh because we see ourselves as superior to somebody else or want to make that person our victim. Rather, the object of our laughter is a sham, an unconscious alibi concocted to outfox the "judge" of the ego. What we are really laughing at, every single time, is ourselves.

John Limon (2000) points out that laughter has a strange intimacy with pain, in that they both produce a sense of obliviousness; according to Limon, laughter and pain are both incorrigible, both are apocalyptic (p. 104), and laughter is "the strongest alternative to shuddering" (p. 137). Similarly, Legman regards laughter as a form of denial, a way of attempting to exorcise neurosis by passing it along to others in the symbolic form of a gasping paroxysm. According to Legman, the mask of laughter is a social disguise, a way of evading other, more painful emotions, such as shock, offense, anger, or terror.

In *No Laughing Matter*, Legman (1975) sees neurotic laughter as at the same time both a denial and a confession. The laughter of the failed clown Harry Greener (West, 1939), like the laughter of the Ik, is a betrayal, a personal revelation, its rhythmic spasms impelled by a drive toward momentary release and relief. This kind of neurotic laughter is a shocking and instinctive kind of autobiographical unveiling. Legman explains that what makes us laugh carries a powerful clue to our own psychological bent and leading neurosis, which we are struggling to unveil and to deny at the same time.

In the examples cited here, neurotic and pathological laughter is apocalyptic because it signifies a momentary revelation. In *No Laughing Matter*,

Legman (1975) regards neurotic laughter as temporarily lifting the veil of social pantomime and parade, allowing the person who laughs to embark on a moment of uncontrolled hostility, in which "all the pretenses can be dropped, and the faked shibboleths and pretended idols can be spat upon, shat upon, derided and destroyed" (p. 743). Moreover, as in the example from *Death in Venice* (Mann, 1912), neurotic laughter can be a form of aggression, especially when it causes its listener/victim to laugh too, perhaps—as in the case of Faye Greener—despite herself. Neurotic laughter often involves a significant element of nervous and guilty enjoyment of the listener's unease. Perhaps part of the function of laughter, as Freud (1905) said of the function of the joke, is to "pass on the blow," with the laugher sloughing off some of his or her anxiety to the listener/victim.

The ostensible gaiety of laughter masks such emotions as fear, hate, sadness, despair, regret, and hostility. In a passage that brings to mind Nietzsche's (1901) description of a joke as "an epitaph on an emotion," Bergson (1911) has a marvelous passage where he describes laughter as being like a remnant of foam left by receding waves on the sandy beach:

> The child who plays hard by, picks up a handful, and, the next moment, is astonished to find that nothing remains in his grasp but a few drops of water, water that is far more brackish, far more bitter, than that of the wave which brought it. Laughter comes into being in the selfsame fashion. It indicates a slight revolt on the surface of social life. It instantly adopts the changing forms of the disturbance. It, also, is a froth with a saline base. Like froth, it sparkles. It is gaiety itself. But the philosopher who gathers a handful to taste may find that the substance is scanty, and the aftertaste bitter [p. 79].

The ancients were the first to comment on the neurotic and pathological nature of certain kinds of human laughter. Plato (370–375 B.C.) considered laughter to be a rational reaction, hiding a lack of self-knowledge. Cicero (55 B.C.) believed that laughter has its spring in some kind of meanness and deformity. Later philosophers came to a similar conclusion. Descartes (1649) believed that the joy that comes from what is good is serious, while that which comes from evil is accompanied by laughter. Spinoza (1677) made the point that a man hates what he laughs at; Baudelaire (1855) called human laughter "satanic" and regarded it as a sign of "fallen humanity." Schopenhauer (1859) thought of laughter as the revenge of the sensuous on the conceptual. "Did they laugh compulsively while pushing the switches at Auschwitz?" wonders Legman (1975), a speculation that leads him to a warning: "Whether with poison gas, phoney electric-chair switches, or jokes, don't let the hysterical laughter fool you" (p. 10). In other words, some kinds of human laughter partake less of catharsis than neurosis; less of the carnival than the apocalypse.

CHAPTER 4

Against Clowns

Robert K. Austin is a volunteer for the Medical Center of Delaware in the Christian Hospital in Wilmington. His role there is as a clown known as "Happy, M.M.D" ("Doctor of Mirth and Merriment") who spends his volunteer hours interacting with patients, visitors, and staff members. He is in full white-face clown makeup and regalia. On one occasion, reports "Happy" in a letter to the journal *Anxiety* (Austin, 1996), he visited a woman in her late 40s or early 50s, who was genuinely frightened by his appearance in her room:

> She assured me that it was nothing personal and that I was probably a very nice person but she had, since childhood, an aversion to and fear of clowns. . . . Throughout the entire time she displayed signs of nervousness and even fear. . . . As I was leaving the room she appeared to relax and even reiterated her position that she did not dislike me personally but was afraid of and disliked all clowns. I truly believe that her behavior bordered on, or was, a true phobia [p. 305].

In an effort to learn more about this experience, Happy performed literature searches at the public and medical libraries. Discovering there was no official term for the condition, he used a Latin dictionary to create the term *ballatrophobia* for "fear of clowns," a term that was subsequently registered at the National Institute for Mental Health. Other terms used for the same condition include *coulrophobia*, as well as the more straightforward *clownophobia*, sometimes also known as *bozophobia*. What seems most surprising about this encounter, however, is not that an adult woman should have harbored a dread of clowns, but that Happy had never previously come across any other clown-haters—or, perhaps more likely, had remained oblivious to their terrors. My intention in this chapter is to use the work of Legman to examine how and why clowns so often inspire horror rather than pleasure and to reveal the truth that many of us have long suspected: there's something inherently evil about the figure of the clown.

Many different Internet sites are currently available for people to discuss their traumatic experiences with what are sometimes referred to as "the stark white-faced ones." These pages include The Anti-Clown Page, The No Clown Zone, The Scary Clown Page, and I Hate Clowns.[1] The section titled "Experiences with Evil Clowns" on The Anti-Clown Page contains numerous examples suggesting that terror of clowns is at least as common as enjoyment of their puerile antics. Typical comments by recovering clown-haters include the following:

> I have to agree that clowns are but sick, twisted caricatures put on earth to fundamentally disturb the impressionable. I have always been disgusted by clowns. Evil, grinning, overly happy, disgusting, acid-inspired freaks of nature.

> The truth is that clowns are, without exception, vicious psychopaths, just waiting for the chance to pounce upon some unsuspecting victim and tear them limb from limb. . . . To this day, if I happen to run into a clown, I break into a cold sweat and have to immediately go to some safe, non-clown place. No, there's nothing funny or nice about clowns.

---

[1] By far the best of these is The Anti-Clown Website at *www.clownz.com*. Similar sites include The No Clown Zone at *www.Ihateclowns.com*; The Scary Clown Page at *www.absurdgallery.com/clowns.html*; and I Hate Clowns, at *www. angelfire.com/nc/worldofNoise/clowns.html*.

I think the appropriate punishment for a clown is to be flattened by one of their props . . . smash them with a giant striped hammer.

One of my earliest memories regarding clowns was watching a parade when I was about 3 or 4 years old. One of the bastards ran up to me, bending down to shove his evil, leering visage right in my face as he laughed a hideous, cackling laugh. I remember curling up in a fetal position and weeping uncontrollably. . . . Now I no longer fear them. The fear of my childhood has developed into a cold, hard hatred.

One day when I was driving from one end of town to the other, I was followed by a clown in his car. Every time I looked in the rear view mirror, the bastard would wave in this slow, weird way and grin. I almost had a heart attack . . . recently a friend told me that her flunking a test was due to the fact that she saw a clown walking along the highway on her way to school. That would be a disturbing sight.

And so it goes on, page after page of vitriol directed against these "monsters" with their "unmistakable psychotic eyes," "plastered grins," and "candy-striped, child-strangling limbs." Terror is perhaps the most commonly expressed reaction to the maniacal antics of clowns— "grinning, honking, dancing, juggling, giggling," "tooting their horns and cracking their jokes." Many of these clown-haters report knowing unpleasant people who turned out to be clowns, as well as clowns who turned out to be unpleasant people:

Imagine my dismay when I found out that a co-worker moonlighted as a clown!!! He was the most mean-spirited sourpuss of a man. Always grumbling and putting people down. A friend moved into a house near mine that I knew was owned by a local clown (since clowns have lawyers, I won't use his "clowning" name—let's call him "Mephisto"). . . . My friend explained, "My dad knows Mephisto from years back through local gun shows."

My innards froze. . . . I mean, look in a gun magazine—there are holsters that can conceal good-sized handguns. Imagine what kind of ordinance is sitting in that clown's baggy pants, acquiring a sheen of sweat, waiting for the day Mephisto finally snaps . . .

Other victims exhibit symptoms of metonymic clown-hatred, that is, a fear of anything associated with the world of clowns—from clown pictures to bulbous scarlet noses and sinister collapsing vehicles, but especially clown dolls—for, after all, the clown's fixed expression itself confuses the human with the uncanny Other that is the inanimate automaton:

I sell real estate in Florida and I go in a lot of houses and see too many knick-knack shelves full of clown figurines that are more creepy than the real thing. What happens to those figurines when the lights go out?

Dolls are bad enough, *clown* dolls are even worse! And worse than that are wind-up clown dolls that go through their routine, their little eyes watching you.

In attempting to account for the origin of their fears, this brave group of assorted clown-haters has various perspectives on the nature of clowns. One describes them as "defensive," another as "perverted." Others find them "sick and twisted," "strangely intense," "loathsome," or "scary and intimidating." Some clowns are simply "losers"; others are "evil incarnate." Cultural critic and self-confessed clown-hater Howard Jacobson (1996) admits to devoting a not inconsiderable portion of his life to hating and avoiding clowns; he concludes that they are "vicious bastards" (p. 105). One thing that Jacobson and his fellow clown-haters often mention is the disparity between what the clown is *supposed* to represent—joy, festivity, and merriment—and the actual sensations of horror and anxiety his presence inevitably evokes. "Yes," admits Jacobson, "the image of a clown *is* sinister, his laughter *is* menacing and deranging, and his merriment *is* a cover for malevolence" (p. 103). With that thick layer of pale, skull-colored makeup and fabricated happy smile disguising his real expression—most likely a leering, vulpine grin—who would not agree that the clown is a malevolent psychotic?

Well, maybe Michael Christianson, founder of the Big Apple Clown Care Unit in New York City and a practicing clown himself, whose lecture on the psychology of positive humor in the face of adversity, given at humor conventions around the country, is titled "Healing Clowns, Clowning Heals: the Red Nose Touches the Heart." Christianson and the rest of the compassionate clowns in the Big Apple Clown Care Unit form part of a long tradition of "healing through humor" that has recently manifested itself in a revival in clowns, clowning, and the circus arts in general. And there's a certain self-conscious "authenticity" about this revival: New Age Clowns, very conscious of their lineage, emphasize their connections to the fools and acrobats of antiquity and to those clowns that have existed under other names throughout the centuries—not to the imposters, out-of-work actors sporting red noses. These contemporary circus artists and humor-healers might perhaps be disturbed by the suggestion that the cheerful smiling clown is not all that he appears to be.

But wait a moment. Isn't it a popular, axiomatic, taken-for-granted irony that clowns are not, in fact, all they appear to be? Few people seem to be disturbed by the homilitic paradox of the "sad clown." In fact, a whole industry of garish Emmett Kelly[2] portraits and tearful Pierrot figurines seems to be founded on this very cliché. Archetypally, the clown "hides his grief," while "playing the fool" as we all know, so that "others may laugh." The sad comedian may supply the crowd with joy but, at least according to popular myth, fails to obtain any lasting happiness in his own life. According to the standard set by the myth of Grimaldi and by the tragic fate of Pagliacci—whose on-stage suicide is at first perceived as clowning by the audience—no clown worth his hooter isn't plagued by internal griefs and anxieties that grant him little mirth of his own.

---

2 It is a little-known fact that Paul Kelly, grandson of Emmett Kelly and himself a professional clown, was convicted of a murder with homosexual overtones. Kelly apparently sought to blame the crime on "Willie," his teary-eyed pathological hobo clown persona, who, he claimed, had "taken him over" in the style of Norman Bates's mother.

Unable to fill the mysterious, aching void in his heart, the clown, or so the story goes, is the saddest of persons off-stage—a man who uses laughter as an ironic mask to conceal the agony of his soul. Jacobson (1996), himself a rather conflicted funnyman, puts it well:

In Pagliacci I saw a reflection of my own condition. A tragic clown. In fact, the phrase was tautologous. What was a *non*-tragic clown? You sat in front of a mirror, you painted your face, and you sobbed in a high tenor voice. That was what you did if you were a clown [p. 149].

This archetypal motif—the impassionate face of the clown who must cry alone—is also, of course, echoed in the narrative structure of most film and television biographies of popular comedians, from *The Eddie Cantor Story* to *Funny Girl*.[3] In all such stories of showbiz clowns, the dominant paradigm is that of the suicidal or near-suicidal comedian who "needs applause like other men need air" and whose jokes conceal an "inner agony" until they "can't hear the laughter any more." According to this mythic formulation, the lives of all truly great clowns are full of suffering, tragedy, and heartbreak; and the clown or comedian is presented as a man (and occasionally a woman) whose troubles can be temporarily suppressed with laughter, but who can never be cured of the misery that sets in whenever the laughter stops. As Grotjahn (1957) puts it, "it is not funny to be funny. For many clowns, 'comedy is no laughing matter' . . . [the clown] will find temporary shelter within a group of admirers—but this is an unsatisfactory solution. Admiration is not love" (p. 48).

Clearly, then, the popular imagination is ready to embrace the cognitive dissonance inherent in the archetype of the miserable clown. At the same time, however, professional clowning is currently a growth industry. The popularity of university courses on the history of clowning, as well as Clown Colleges, "Humor Therapy" regimens, and organizations like Michael Christianson's sinister-sounding "Clown Care Unit," suggests

---

3 Other important biopics in the same line include *The Buster Keaton Story* (1957), *Can You Hear the Laughter? The Freddie Prinze Story* (1979), and, of course, *Lenny* (1974).

a powerful resistance to acknowledge that the clown, even if privately unhappy, could ever be anything but helpful and good. And yet, if the comments by the traumatized clown haters who frequent the Anti-Clown Page are anything to go by, America's love affair with these kitschy, teary-eyed buffoons has its underside in a deep-seated loathing of anything to do with the clown.

Does anybody think of clowns as sad and noble any more, even in a shabby genteel kind of a way? Or when people think "clown," do they automatically think "evil"? "A few years ago," writes Happy, "after the film *It* was shown (the villain was a clown), members of the pre-teen group pretended to be frightened by clowns, but this was a short-lived condition that soon passed" (p. 305). As Happy suggests, one popular current of thought relates recent outbreaks of clown-hating to the presentation of creepy clowns in contemporary film and television productions.

Cruel clowns play a prominent role in the movies *Carnival of Blood* (1972), *The Clown Murders* (1975), *Poltergeist* (1982), *Out of the Dark* (1988), *Clownhouse* (1988), and, of course, *Killer Klowns from Outer Space* (1988). Other films feature clowns as down-on-their-luck losers, like the eponymous cynical boozehound in *Shakes the Clown* (1992), or the antiheroes of *Quick Change* (1990), and *Funland* (1989). Filmmaker Tim Burton incorporates nasty clowns into most of his movies, including the bike-napping funnymen of *Peewee's Big Adventure* (1985), the twisted carnival creations of *Beetlejuice* (1988), the menacing joker and his gang of grinning thugs in *Batman* (1989), the kidnapping crime crew known as the "Red Triangle Circus Gang" of *Batman Returns* (1992), and "the clown with the tear-away face who's here in a flash and gone without a trace" in *The Nightmare Before Xmas* (1993).

Malevolent clowns have appeared in television episodes of *Scooby Doo*, *Fantasy Island*, and *The Twilight Zone*. Recent bad Bozos on the small screen include the kid-hating Krusty on *The Simpsons*; Crazy Joe Davola, the abusive Pagliacci clown who tormented Jerry on *Seinfeld*; and the alcoholic Chuckles on *The Mary Tyler Moore Show*, who ends up getting crushed by an elephant while dressed as a peanut.

One of the most frightening of evil clowns to appear on the small screen is the homicidal pedophile Pennywise in the television adaptation of Stephen King's (1990) epic novel, *It*. This novel is the story of an evil clown who resides in the sewer system of Derry, Maine. Pennywise reflects every social and familial horror known to contemporary America: racism, gay bashing, child abuse, wife beating, animal torture, parental neglect, and, perhaps most insidious of all, total indifference. Feeding off the children of the town, Pennywise emerges from the sewers once every 27 years to wreak havoc until seven child outcasts known as "the losers" gather together to fight back against their hideous, red-nosed adversary.

According to cultural critic Mark Dery (1999), the figure of the evil clown (or the "Bozopath," as Dery calls him) encapsulates the Have-A-Nice-Day/Make-My-Day dualism that typifies postwar western culture, particularly in America. "We're not happy and sad," says Dery, "we're happy and violent" (p. 79). Makers of scary Halloween masks now regularly include skull-faced jesters and grinning Bozopaths in their popular repertoire. A number of contemporary artists, especially Robert Williams and R. K. Sloane, specialize in depictions of amputee clowns, cannibal clowns, and circus serial killers. Legman and other folklorists, including David Cornwell and Sandy Hobbs (1988), have drawn attention to the prevalence of the creepy clown in recent urban legends and the ubiquity in the last 15 years of "Killer Clown" scares, often in poverty-stricken urban areas.

In September 1991, report Cornwell and Hobbs, police in Strathclyde, Scotland, issued a press release appealing for information regarding "two persons dressed in clown outfits, using a blue-coloured Ford Transit type van, approaching children and offering sweets" (p. 115). Cornwell and Hobbs add that two months later, a similar scare was related in Glasgow, and, in October 1995, police in London were looking for a hitman dressed as a clown, wearing a pink wig, red nose, and false teeth and with a gun nestling in his bouquet. Around the same time, sandwich-board advertisers in Edmonton, Alberta, Canada were banned from dressing up as clowns owing to a series of clown-directed drive-by shootings.

As Legman (1968) has pointed out, however, contemporary legends like these are seldom a product of single causes and incidents and need to be seen as part of a much older and wider phenomenon. Cornwell and Hobbs have traced a long history of phantom clown sightings in other parts of the world and at other times. And, of course, the history of Western literature was shadowed by sinister fools and nasty jesters—from Mr. Punch to Poe's murderous Hop-Frog—long before Stephen King's Pennywise slithered out of the toy closet.

The word clown derives from the Old Norse *klunni*, meaning loutish, cognate with the Danish *kluntet*, meaning clumsy or maladroit. It is important to remember that the type of clown that has become the generic "clown" of 20th century popular culture—the red-nosed, grinning Bozo—is actually a version of the August, a very specific and particular type of clown. Other kinds of clowns, including the whitefaced clown, the Hobo, the Pierrot, the Harlequin, and the character clown, have developed in other ways and in other forms. With the advent of industrialization in Europe, for instance, France's beloved Pierrot clown, the sensitive soul in whiteface, was given a darker side: the Pierrot-ombre, who wore all black, often a businessman's suit, as a parody of the bourgeoisie. These Pierrots could be downright vicious, often resorting to theft and murder to get ahead in the world. But the figure most of us think of when we imagine a circus clown is the August, with his baggy trousers, red nose, and painted face.[4] The August, however, is a very recent type of clown; it has existed for little more than 100 years. Over the last century, as Legman (1968) notes, clowns have usually worked in pairs or troupes, with one white-faced clown and one or more Augusts.[5]

---

[4] Acknowledgments are gratefully exended to Mark Best for pointing this out, as well as for his many other insightful comments on an earlier draft of this chapter.

[5] The word August comes from the German, meaning silly or stupid. The Augusts that worked on their own were originally called carpet clowns, although this term has more recently been used to describe fill-in circus clowns who come on to keep the audience amused between acts while the ring hands move things around in readiness for the next act. Incidentally, Legman and his first wife, Beverley Keith, provided the original English translation of Alfred Jarry's *Ubi Roi* (1953), one of the first absurdist plays ever written, featuring the grotesque monarchical character known as Pere Ubu. A combination of Punch and Macbeth, Pere Ubu was the ultimate white-trash clown who trampled on everything in his attempt to become all-powerful. Apparently, Jarry himself dressed as a sort of deranged Pierrot to introduce the first, and last, performance of the play to a soon-to-be-scandalized Parisian audience.

Legman (1968) explains that the historical origins of all contemporary versions of the clown go back to the wandering musicians, beggars,
tumblers, minstrels, and acrobats who roamed the continent after the fall
of the Roman Empire. Their groups included lepers, the blind, wandering prostitutes, quack doctors, paralytics, and amputees. Later on, according to Legman, these itinerant entertainers were given a fixed habitat at
court. Sometimes the court fool was a brilliant, witty man, but more often
than not he was insane or deformed, deaf or mute, diseased or blind.
Others were carnival sleight-of-hand tricksters or the "semicriminal" type
of jester embodied by the 15th century German clown Tyl Eulenspiegel,
"whose jests and merry pranks," as Legman (1975) points out, "are the
most scatological of all such jests" (p. 414). Also, J. E. Cirlot (1971) notes
that the Fool and the Clown "play the part of scapegoats in the ritual sac-
rifice of humans" in "the period immediately preceding history" (p. 162).

In Europe, traditional carnival antics generally drew attention to the
animal aspects of the human body. As Legman (1968) explains, the
medieval religious festival of the Feast of Fools, which derived from the
Roman Saturnalia, was full of dark masquerading, indecent posturing,
licentious behavior, anal aggressions, and dime-a-dozen obscenities.
Legman (1968) describes how masked clowns at the Feast of Fools would
assault each other with their flatus and feces, throw filth and ordure about
in public, and openly perform unusual sex acts on one another. As a version of carnival, the medieval Feast of Fools celebrated the basic functions of what Bakhtin (1968) refers to as the "lower bodily stratum" (p. 312)
—urine and excrement were glorified, and the body revealed in all its
grotesque monstrosity. Carnival, according to Bakhtin, is a time when the
official and sacred order is mocked and inverted and the unofficial and
profane are worshipped and enthroned: the king becomes clown, and the
clown becomes king.

Although, as Legman (1968) points out, such rituals seem to have
died out by the beginning of the 16th century, the standardized clowns
of the Greeks and Romans were revived in the Italian *Commedia dell'Arte*
during the 17th century, and certain of the original classical characters
were taken over by Hanswurst[6] and Harlequin, who eventually became

---

6 According to Tarachow (1951), "the anal birth of the clown in *Geburt des*

the many different European clown types of today. In fact, the cane wielded by the modern-day whitefaced Bozo is a descendent of the wooden "goosing sword" manipulated by the comedy *braggadocio* or bully, the phallically posturing street clown of the *Commedia dell'Arte* (Legman, 1975, p. 142), who entertained the public with ribaldries in true Rabelasian style.

The *braggadocio* and his swaggering fellow clowns each, of course, had his own individual brand of grotesquerie. No performance of the *Commedia dell'Arte* would be complete without the antics of Il Dottore, with his bushy lambswool eyebrows; the fluttering, gesticulating Pantalone; Brighella, with his wiry animal-hair moustache; or Il Capitano, with his unambiguously phallic nose. And just as the role of the clown today attracts some rather questionable characters, so the most famous players of the *Commedia dell'Arte* may not have been the devout and consummate *artistes* that the ballyhoo surrounding their stage performances generally declared them to be. Jacobson (1996) tells a revealing anecdote about Jean-Gaspard Deburau, the celebrated 19th century Pierrot of the Funambules in Paris, who apparently, off-stage, was a homicidal maniac:

> On one occasion when he was out taking the Paris air with his wife, a street boy taunted him. . . . Deburau raised his stick in retaliation and struck the boy dead, returning to the Funambules a few hours later where he performed as usual, without any perceptible diminution of authority or variation of style, the part of Pierrot [p. 86].

Such malignancy is not surprising when we remember that the *Commedia del'Arte* developed from the Feast of Fools, whose protagonists were closely related to minor imps and demons. Their costumes, for example, were quite similar, though generally the demon was erect where the clown was droopy. Sidney Tarachow (1951) explains how the imps in medieval farces would leave the stage to mingle with the audience for the dual purpose of terrifying and amusing—just as modern

---

Hanswursten is characteristic: it should be noted that the doctor who gives the enema is dark, hooded and almost masked. The 'mother' is also dark and there is a suggestion of facial masking" (p. 182).

clowns in the circus do, who inevitably accomplish the same double result, especially with children (p. 181). Moreover, in paintings by Dührer and Holbein, the Fool and Death are interchangeable, sometimes subsumed into Death the Fool, a skeleton in a jester's cap and motley. The medieval fool was also the agent of death; William Willeford (1969) points to "the similarities between the Fool as Jester and the figure of Revenger in many Elizabethan and Jacobean plays" (p. 89).

In the context of American cultural history, however, the clown emerges from a different tradition. While the Native American plains tribes had their own various manifestations of the Trickster figure, the main clown type of non-Native Americans was not the August, as it was in Europe, but the character clown. Prior to the Civil War, character clowns, like the famous Dan Rice, were mimics and satirists who specialized in commenting humorously on contemporary political events. After the war ended, however, one particular style of character clown came into prominence: the Hobo. Eric Lott (1993) describes how the Hobo figure was originally based on the blackface minstrel clowns (hence the exaggerated white mouths) who portrayed the figures of African Americans made homeless by the ravages of the Civil War.

Lott explains that the Hobo character clown is a distinctly American invention, with his tattered hat, huge white mouth, three days' growth of beard, torn clothes, and cartoon alcoholic's big red nose. This down-on-his-luck Hobo eventually developed into the miserable vagabond clown epitomized by Emmett Kelly's immensely popular Weary Willie character and later by Charlie Chaplin's sentimental Little Tramp. It seems ironic that such mawkishly appealing personalities had their roots in the miseries of poverty and oppression and the disfigurements of alcoholism and venereal disease.

This genealogy, however, does little to explain why the whitefaced August has emerged as the modern generic type of clown and why this particular embodiment of the figure causes so much terror, even to those who are not necessarily aware of its historical links to destruction and to evil. Whatever his antecedents, there seems to be something about this specific form of clown that is *intrinsically* scary. In Angela Carter's (1984) novel *Nights at the Circus*, the psychopathic clown Buffo the Great, discussing this paradox with a crowd of his colleagues, explains that there is no element of the *voluntary* in clowning:

> Often, d'you see, we take to clowning when all else fails. Under these impenetrable disguises of wet white, you might find, were you to look, the features of those who were once proud to be visible. You find there, per example, the *aerialiste* whose nerve has failed; the bare-back rider who took one tumble too many; the juggler whose hands shake so, from drink or sorrow, that he can no longer keep his balls in the air. And then what is left but the white mask of poor Pierrot, who invites the laughter that would otherwise come unbidden. The child's laughter is pure until he first laughs at a clown [p. 119].

Many clown-haters draw attention to the permanent facial expression of the white-faced clown as particularly terrifying. "I don't know why I find clowns so frightening," comments one clown-hater:

> I think it has to do with how happy they are, almost hysterically, and it's all too easy to imagine that smile suddenly fade away, to be replaced with a hating sneer. The way they act is so unnatural, that you *know* it's false. It's a false mask, it's a false act, and the *imagination* goes haywire about what the clown is *really* like. You begin to wonder what they're really up to.

Others make similar points about this transparent artifice, which tends to give rise to the creeping suspicion that the clown in his daily life is an embittered alcoholic, sexual predator, or spooky child-killer. "The permanent facial expression of a clown represents an unstable mind that cannot act like a normal mind," observes another clown-hater. "Consider the clown as a possible victim of multiple personality syndrome. The face says one thing, but the mind is drifting somewhere else."

And while the mask of the modern clown is not as extreme as those of antiquity—which, as Legman (1968) points out, were characterized by enormous lolling tongues, like the gargoyles that decorated medieval churches—the facial makeup is the most vivid and significant index of the contemporary whitefaced clown. In the professional clowning mafia, in fact, so much importance is attached to this part of the costume that, once the clown has designed his own facial mask, no other clown may imitate it (or else . . .). Again, this fixed, stylized mask evokes the themes of mental illness. Tarachow (1951) observes that "certain patients, especially obsessive-compulsives and deeply masochistic ones, express many of their aggressions through facial grimacing" (p. 776). "The code of the circus permits no copying, no change," claims Buffo the Great in Angela Carter's (1984) *Nights at the Circus*:

> However much the face of Buffo may appear identical to Grik's face, or to Grok's face, or to Coco's face, or Pozzo's, Bimbo's faces, or to the face of any other joey, carpet clown or August, it is, all the same, a fingerprint of authentic dissimilarity, a genuine expression of my own autonomy. And so my face eclipses me. I have become this face which is not mine, and yet I chose it freely [p. 122].

The costume of the clown is also more than a trifle disturbing. His outfit is supposed to be "funny," presumably because it is assumed to poke fun at authority by presenting a ludicrous imitation of pomposity and dignity—the oversized necktie, dangling braces, baggy pants, gigantic shoes, and so on. In effect, however, such accoutrements are versions of the medieval fool's many droopy symbols of castration and impotence (and symbolism, as Legman [1968] says, is a form of social expurgation: "one says in symbols what one dare not say, or cannot bear to say in fact" [p. 609]).[7] Grotjahn (1957) puts it very well:

> The circus clown wears an enormous, outsized necktie. One end is much larger than the other and hangs down almost to the knees like an oversized but empty scrotum. It constantly has to be stuffed back into the outrageously large, baggy pants, which again

---

[7] Legman (1975) explains how such disparate arts as the act of the feint in feinting and symbolism (both sexual and other) are related to metonymy and synechdoche in that, in all cases, one thing is said (or done) but is intended to suggest another.

are so big that the contents seem to be ridiculously small and lost. Symbols of the limp, impotent and ridiculous penis are repeated in many variations [p. 92].

Grotjahn argues that, in this costume of impotence, the clown comes to symbolize the father—once big and fearful, but now depreciated, castrated and ridiculed (p. 93).

Tarachow (1951) makes the point that the clown's ludicrous and exaggerated costume—oversized shoes, overpadded shoulders, prominent gloves, big red nose—relates to his neurotic and perverted measures to attempt to deny castration anxieties. Tarachow concludes that "the circus is occupied with the same problems . . . that occupy fetishists and transvestites" (p. 176). The fighting and tumbling of circus clowns seems connected in a significant way with "the ostentatious flirting with sickness and accident" regarded by Legman (1968) as a sign of overt hostility (p. 604).

Perhaps more than anything else, however, clowns are scary because they seem constantly on the verge of falling "out of context," just as a madman constantly fears the loss of boundary between himself and the world. At a certain distance, the clown may be quite bearable, but if you get too close, his "funny" face can appear hideously disfigured—just as, says Grotjahn (1957), to the child in the arms of the department store Santa Claus, "the smiling bearded face and colorful costume become a grotesque phantom from his nightmares" (p. 468). One clown-hater reports being particularly disturbed "when their unpainted skin pops out from a pant leg or collar." And while everybody knows the horrible feeling of trepidation that accompanies the onslaught of an oncoming clown—the pressure to acknowledge his presence and *play the game*, however disinclined one might be to do so[8]—even worse is the sudden appearance of the clown who's capered just a little too far from the circus ring.

Of course, once anyone is removed from the place in which one ordinarily performs, that person then becomes scary or absurd—consider the impact of a surgeon turning up at a child's birthday party, or a priest in a topless bar. Context is always important, but, because clowns are tra-

---

[8] A terror that often extends to mimes and all other costumed characters, especially those which prowl around American theme parks.

ditionally so closely connected with pleasure and delight, especially the pleasure and delight of children, there seems to be something particularly terrifying about a clown's turning up in the *wrong place*. Many writers, scholars, and philosophers have commented on the uncanny nature of the out-of-context clown.

One contemporary artist who deals with precisely this subject is Bruce Nauman, the creator of a video installation project called *Clown Torture* (1997). The installation consists of two videotapes of segments depicting clowns in frustrating or embarrassing situations; the tapes play simultaneously and continuously. Nauman sees the clown as emblematic of the figure of the artist in contemporary society: one who is separated from the everyday world and thereby permitted to do and say things that would not ordinarily be tolerated but who, at the same time, is expected to fulfill collective social fantasies. The tension the artist feels between his identity as a private person and his role as a public figure informs the video segment "Clown Taking a Shit," which Nauman describes as a form of "clown torture."

> If you think of times when [being an artist] is difficult as mental constipation, then the image of a clown taking a shit (not in a household bathroom but in a public restroom—a gas station, an airport—places where privacy is qualified or compromised) can make a useful parallel.⁹

Intrinsically, the clown embodies the ambiguous, frighteningly elusive nature of the boundary between funny and horrifying, between sanity and madness. "What dark compulsion drives these men to hide behind their painted-on smiles and big rubber noses?" ponder Dave Louapre and Dan Sweetman (1989). "What madness turns a man into a clown?" (p. 24).

One clown-hater remarks that clowns remind her of "mental patients," and this is a very interesting observation. In earlier times, visiting the local lunatic asylum was a common pastime; there was great amusement

---

⁹ "Clown Torture" employs two 20-inch color monitors, four speakers, two video projectors and four videotapes. It was exhibited in New York at the Museum of Modern Art in April 1995. This quotation is from the catalogue.

to be had in watching the inmates rave, gibber, and masturbate. Of course, as psychotherapist Eugene Daniels Jr. (1973) observes, "Remarking on this clown-like aspect of the madman . . . has fallen into disrepute; . . . mental hospital staff are discouraged from viewing patients . . . as clowns" (p. 466). And yet it is important and justifiable to examine the roots of these associations, however offensive they may seem to us today.

One of the most frightening aspects of the out-of-place clown is that he reminds us of the frail boundaries of our mental health and threatens us with the loss of the rational, adult relationships we have established with one another and with the everyday world. The out-of-place clown is also terrifying because his presence cannot help but make us suspect, like Thomas Mann's (1954) Felix Krull, that circus clowns—those "cavorting hybrids"—may not actually be humans in disguise at all, as they try to make us believe; they may, in fact, be a completely unique species—cultural, even *biological* freaks:

> Are they really human, those . . . fun-makers with little red hands, little thin-shod feet, red wigs under conical felt hats, their impossible lingo, their handstands, their stumbling and falling over everything, their mindless running to and fro? . . . Are these ageless, half-grown sons of absurdity . . . human at all? With their chalk-white faces and utterly preposterous facial expressions—triangular eyebrows and deep perpendicular grooves in their cheeks under the reddened eyes, impossible noses, mouths twisted up at the corners into insane smiles . . .—are they, I repeat, human beings, men that could conceivably find a place in everyday life? [p. 274].

The figure of the malevolent clown is familiar not only to narrative and fiction, but also to the realm of dreams, imagination, and, sometimes, hallucination, thus confirming the significance of its role in human consciousness. Psychologists L. E. Braddock and R. N. S. Heard (1986) report the case study of a 22-year-old single man suffering from various neurological maladies. He hallucinated a series of life-sized, three-dimensional, solid, moving clowns. These clowns had long arms and pointed hats and dressed in a black-and-white harlequin pattern. When the patient was

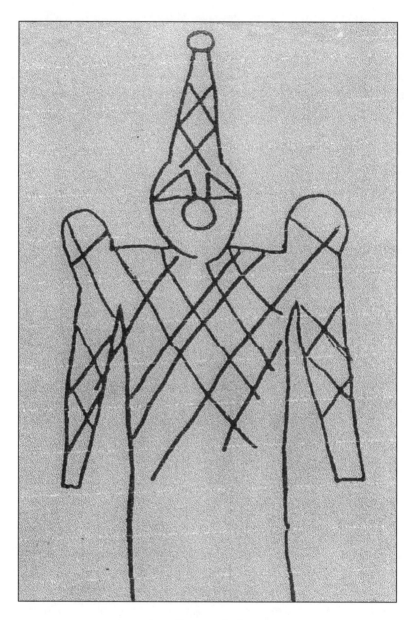

Figure 1: Hallucinated Clown Image

asked to draw them, he realized that they had "no legs" (p. 264). After a while, the clowns started laughing in an unfriendly way, and the patient felt as if "they were hitting him on the head" (p. 264). Unsurprisingly, these malicious jesters left him with a thumping headache (see Figure 1).

The circus antics of clowns, especially when represented in dream or hallucination, can produce great anxiety, particularly when a "dignified" clown is pitted against a sillier one. The crazy games of this mismatched pair can evoke in observers the traumatic split between childhood and adulthood, reminding them of the fears and conflicts of the latency period. French psychoanalysts Soulé (1988) and Chervet (1996) have discussed how, in such typical vignettes, the clown comes to represent the self, whose embodiment as austere, mature adult is mocked by the childhood personality and its fatuous monkeyshines. The adult is reduced, destabilized, and desexualized (castrated) by the child, a process that articulates fears of regression and disintegration. This presentation of self in two simultaneous modalities is typical, according to Chervet and Soulé, of anxiety-evoking scenarios.

The horror evoked by the out-of-place clown is perfectly epitomized by the statement, often attributed to film actor Lon Chaney, that "the essence of true horror" is "a clown at midnight." A clown, or so the saying goes, is funny in the circus ring, but imagine opening a door at midnight and finding the same clown standing there in the darkness. Coincidentally, such a terrifying encounter was described to Chicago police by 19-year-old David Cram, who as Cahill (1986) describes, opened his door well after midnight on August 23 1976, only to be confronted by a 230 lb. clown wearing a dark, sharply pointed smile. The clown in question was Pogo, better known as John Wayne Gacy.

How many clown-haters were *really* surprised when, in December 1978, the killer of 33 young boys in Chicago turned out to be Pogo the Clown? In 1975, John Wayne Gacy joined the Jolly Joker Club, part of a Moose Lodge in River Grove, Chicago. The Jolly Jokers performed for children at Easter, Christmas, and Halloween, at hospitals, parades, and holiday parties. Gacy had a costume made for himself, devised his own makeup, and chose his own clown name, Pogo, because, he claimed, he was Polish and "on the go all the time." Later on, when he worked as the contractor for an ice-cream company in Chicago that offered 33 flavors,[10] he also began to work as "the 33 Flavors Clown"—a morbid irony, since this was exactly the number of young boys he was eventually convicted of killing.

John Wayne Gacy loved clowns. One of his favorite songs, he claimed, was the sappy, tear-jerking ditty, "Send in the Clowns." After starting work as Pogo, he got rid of his collection of bullfight figurines and started collecting clown paintings. Apparently, he especially liked pictures of sad-faced clowns. "To me," claimed Gacy in an interview with author Tim Cahill (1986), "clowning is a way of relaxation. . . . You regress to your childhood, you're able to relax and you can be goofy if you want to and you still have a disguise" (p. 84).

But Pogo was always something of a sinister clown. Gacy claimed that Pogo allowed him to do things he would never do without his clown face on, since, as he soon realized, few people ever question what clowns do. In a crowd, he claimed to Cahill, he would run up to a strange woman and "honk her boobs" ("Nobody ever said shit. 'Oh well, it's okay, he's a clown'" . . . "You know clowns can get away with murder" [p. 88]). "If you're going to clown for children," claimed William Kunkle, the prosecutor in the Gacy case, in a television interview, "you use very smooth, round makeup. John Gacy used very *pointy* makeup around the mouth and the eyes, which really makes it very sinister . . . makes it really the embodiment of evil." Moreover, at least according to Cahill, Pogo also occasionally liked to harm and abuse the children he was supposed to be "entertaining":

> He'd pinch the kid on the cheek, like clowns will do, only he pinched hard, so that it hurt and he could see the pain in the child's eyes. Smiling, and whispering so that no one else but the child could hear, Pogo would rasp "get your ass away from me, you little motherfucker." And then he'd be up, capering around, a perfect fool, putting people and distance between himself and a suddenly sobbing child: Pogo smiling his dark, pointed smile [p. 150].

---

[10] According to Legman (1968), America's obsession with ice cream is a reflection of "the remarkable overemphasis on milk drinks and refections" in contemporary society—"one of the most noticeable aspects of the breast-return orality of American adults" (p. 572).

As far as we know, Gacy never committed any of his murders while dressed as Pogo, but he certainly tried to kill David Cram after turning up at his home in the middle of the night in his clown-suit. In his Pogo costume, Gacy proceeded to get drunk, pop pills, and smoke a few joints before tying Cram to the bed in the guise of showing him a "handcuff trick" and attempting to rape him. But Cram managed to kick the evil clown in the head, smearing his greasepaint and knocking him unconscious, giving the boy enough time to reach the keys and unfasten himself.

On the night of Gacy's execution at Statesville Correctional Center in Chicago, May 10, 1994, a number of angry clowns held vigil outside the prison. Eagerly anticipating Gacy's death, they were angry at his soiling the face of clowndom. Many held up cards containing vitriolic messages of support for the execution: "Clowns Should Delight Kids, Not Murder Them"; "No More Tears for This Clown"; "See You in Hell, Clown."

Since his execution, Gacy's paintings have been fetching high prices on the international art market. "My art imitates parts—but not all—of my life," wrote Gacy in one of his many letters from prison, selected and compiled by Gacy with C. Ivor McLelland (1995). "Generally, the darkest corners are eerily absent, lost in riotous colors and often whimsical themes" (p. 11). His "Hi-Ho Series," pictures of Snow White and the Seven Dwarfs, is especially popular with collectors, as are his crude, cartoonlike portraits of Elvis and Christ. But most valuable of all are his clown portraits. These paintings include a picture of Pogo's buddy Patches, another of Pogo himself, and an empty chair with a clown costume draped over it. Perhaps the most haunting of all his pictures, however, is Gacy's "Decomposing Clown" (see Figure 2). This ghoulish skull in ruffled collar and clown hat bears a remarkable similarity to the skull-headed jesters of Holbein's *Death and the Lady* (1490) (see Figure 3).

As the Gacy case demonstrates, there is no concealing—not even from a child—the grotesque, undisciplined aggression that is the secret of the vitality of even the most inane and innocuous clown. "Certain patients," observes Tarachow (1951), in a description that perfectly fits John Wayne Gacy, "mostly men with strong, unresolved, sadomasochistic tendencies and femininity, fear failure in genital aggressions and substitute it for comic aggressions and a debased, clowning type of exhibitionism" (p. 172). The Gacy case is also a good example of the way in which violent emotions

Figure 2: John Wayne Gacy, *Decomposing Clown*

Figure 3: Hans Holbein, *Death and the Lady*

such as fear and nervous strain can easily become eroticized—which is "precisely the reason for the popularity of ghost-stories and horror-films, and other sadistic entertainments such as bull-fights" (Legman, 1968, p. 645).[11]

According to Freud (1900), the most powerful symbols in our lives are those which fuse conflicts and embrace enigmas. Ambivalence, polarity, duplicity, and dualism are qualities that in psychoanalysis often denote phantoms created by unconscious fears—and they are also, according to Mircea Eliade (1974), characteristics of the sacred.

The ambiguity of the clown can be disturbing to those whose minds are used to operating within the limits of logic and rationality. The intuitive clown-hater, however, perceives that comedy is just another way of opening the doors to horror and that the clown is also, always, the devil. It is impossible to know all the secret connections between these two figures, or to understand all their complexities. But, then, to reveal the clown's terrible secrets would be to lose the intrinsic mystery and fantasy of this sinister, striking, enigmatic figure.[12]

---

[11] "In cultures that plan to survive," concludes Legman, "this connection cannot be exploited" (p. 645).

[12] On a personal note, while researching this subject, I observed a workshop at Indiana University designed to help university undergraduates "discover their inner clown." After the meeting, I discussed my research briefly with the workshop leader, a professional clown apparently trained at circus school, and asked if he would be kind enough to give me his thoughts on an early draft of this chapter. He agreed and seemed quite interested in my work. Two days later, however, I received my paper back in the mail, accompanied by a vitriolic note from the offended clown, which began: "To say I found your paper disturbing is an understatement." Afraid to provoke the wrath of an angry clown any further than necessary, I let the matter drop. Less than a month later, however, I found myself at a dinner party seated directly opposite this very same clown—without his makeup—who turned out to be the brother-in-law of a colleague. He proved friendly enough after a few glasses of wine, but I detected a note of barely suppressed hostility in his overloud laughter that only confirmed my first suspicions and increased my already deep mistrust of anyone who feels compelled to take on the role of the clown.

CHAPTER 5

Against Stand-Up

Do we fear other people so much that we must mark *their* pain with laughter, our own with tears?

—Trevor Griffiths, *Comedians*

The modern stand-up comedian is, in many ways, a contemporary version of the clown or jester, the traditional court fool. Folklore scholar Orrin Klapp (1950) has argued that, in early societies, the antic fool was valuable and necessary because he served important social functions. He used comic relief to upset decorum, for example, to ease social routine, and to enhance group cohesion by encouraging mockery as a social sanction. The traditional fool was also an educator, providing a negative example in literature and folklore.

In his discussion of the nature of clowning, psychoanalyst Joseph Levine (1961) regards the traditional fool as expressing, in an appropriately controlled form, the repressed aspects of a particular society. The fool offered an outlet for public anxieties about those events, situations, and taboos that people found most frightening and difficult to deal with. The fool was thereby responsible for handling something "not proper" in society—something that Levine describes as "embarrassing, astonishing and shocking" (p. 76).

This character functioned, therefore, as a kind of scapegoat, manifesting (and often being punished for) the deep-seated antisocial urge to say what we truly mean instead of being diplomatically polite. The genuine fool, like the lunatic or village idiot, had a socially sacrosanct ability to tell the truth and to blame this habit on his folly or madness. The fool went way beyond the bounds of traditional decorum and was regularly ridiculed and despised for doing so. Only the genuine fool was allowed, as Legman (1975) puts it, "the id expression of what he really wants" (p. 177).

At the same time, however, the traditional fool—the *schlemiel*, who, according to Yiddish folklore, trips over his own feet and tumbles backward into heaven—is identified with the protracted childhood we would all love to live and somehow shows it to be sacrosanct and above danger. As Legman notes, the fool is saved by his folly, and ultimately proves wiser than his persecutors: "Only the Trickster or Fool survives—God's Fool, he who has been 'touched'—saved precisely by his folly-that-is-wisdom, and that is the wishful dream of every child" (p. 190). But it is very important to remember that the fool is also what Legman (1968) describes as

a "jerk" (*jerk-off*, or masturbator, traditionally insane) or "schmuck," actually a South-Slavic term for a fool, *smok*, but identified with the Judeo-German *schmuck*, jewel, a euphemism for the penis as the principal ornament of a man, and very much a pejorative term, both in Yiddish and in English, when applied to the man himself [p. 716].

In this chapter, I use the work of Legman to understand the personal and cultural psychology of the contemporary stand-up comic—the modern-day version of the traditional fool—and consider the complex and troubling relationship between the stand-up and his or her audience. To begin with, Legman reminds us of the way Freud focused powerfully on the personal intentions and functions of the joke-teller and on his or her specific (if unconscious) motivations and satisfactions. Only when the motives of the stand-up comedian are understood can we locate the secret connections between the comic and the response of the audience. We also need to investigate the motives behind audience applause, which is not always as unambiguous as it may appear to be. Victor Hugo (1869) describes "that form of isolation known as public applause" (p. 337). And applause, it has often been claimed, is the beginning of abuse.

According to popular belief, the stand-up comedian, like the clown, is regarded as a person whose only source of gratification comes from making people laugh, a person who thrives on public attention and, off-stage, is miserable, lonely, and embittered. This stereotype is a staple of movies about the comedy business and is most memorably incarnated in characters like the disgruntled Jerry Langford in Martin Scorsese's *King of Comedy* (1983), the desperate Steven Gold in David Seltzer's *Punchline*, and the doleful Tommy Fawkes in Peter Chelsom's *Funny Bones* (1995). Stand-up comics are also presented as anguished, self-destructive losers in most biopics set in the world of comedy, especially Charles Vidor's 1957 film about Joe E. Lewis, *The Joker's Wild* and, most memorably, Bob Fosse's *Lenny* (1974).

These blistering portraits of stand-up comedians are based on the folkloric belief that, at a deep level, all funnymen are miserable inside. Legman (1975) refers to "the obvious *need* that the performer has for the audience, whose presence and response (that shriving laughter!) are a pre-condition of the joke-teller's inspiration, the same mechanism where a bird soars on rising currents of air" (p. 35).

Like many stereotypes, however, this characterization of the stand-up comic as privately unhappy is not entirely groundless. Samuel Janus, a psychologist interested in the personalities of stand-up comedians, spent 10 years interviewing 76 subjects, including, among others, George Burns, Milton Berle, and Sid Caesar. Janus (1975) concluded that most humor emerges from depression and intense alienation and that the comic skills of stand-up comedians begin as a defense mechanism to ward off aggression and the hostility of others.

A journalist friend of mine who regularly covers "Jest for Laughs," the Annual Comedy Festival in Montreal, describes the atmosphere there as one of great bitterness, generated in part by nightly stand-up performances notable for their barely repressed anger and jealousy. Sitcom producers and club organizers will often attend the festival on the lookout for new television stars or regular acts for their clubs. Inevitably, this search leads to all kinds of dark envy and backstabbing, enhancing the general feeling of psychopathy in the air. The morning seminars, according to my friend, are sparsely attended, since most people seem to be sleeping off hangovers caused by evenings of binge drinking. Every night the clubs are packed with miserable, hostile comedians drowning their sorrows in booze and repeating the same jokes and stories every few hours to any sucker who will listen. In the early hours of the morning, wherever you go, you can spot a lineup of once-almost-famous, aged Borscht Belt comics leaning drunkenly against the bar, their toupees askew, still high from their moment in the spotlight, sharing age-old showbiz tales with young comedians naive enough to be impressed.

In fact, by their own reckoning, most comedians *are* miserable people. Perhaps even more than any other group in show business, comedians—and not just stand-ups—are notoriously unhappy in their private lives. Comics who have gone public with their battles against depression are too numerous to mention; recent notables within their ranks include Woody Allen, Roseanne Barr, Rodney Dangerfield, Benny Hill, and John Cleese. Similarly, the list of comedians who have confessed to drug or alcohol addictions is virtually endless; familiar names include Buster Keaton, Jackie Gleason, Robin Williams, Richard Pryor, Eddie Murphy, and Paula Poundstone. For many—Lenny Bruce, John Belushi, Chris Farley, Sam Kinison, and Bill Hicks—these addictions eventually proved fatal. British comedian Peter Cook sought psychiatric help when he realized, he confessed to a friend, he had been "doing funny voices" for so long that he wasn't sure who he was any more.[1] Richard Pryor attempted suicide; radio comic Tony Hancock eventually took his own life.

Autobiographies of stand-up comedians all seem to tell the same sad stories, all of them about people who never liked themselves, no matter what they did, until they finally learned to relieve the pain with laughter and applause. The more successful and accomplished they become, the more fraudulent they feel, and any brief setback in their career leads to depression and abuse. Then, after years of addiction and abandon, they finally achieve a breakthrough in the form of an emotional relationship, spiritual revelation, or public acknowledgment of their addiction. Only in the final stage of life do they learn to forgo the dubious satisfactions

---

[1] This spontaneous use of different voices may bear some relation to jokes involving disembodied utterances, often attributed to, say, a parrot or ventriloquist's dummy. According to Legman, such voices can represent either the unleashed id or the superego—the internalized conscience.

of public applause and learn to live a fulfilling life with no need for public adulation or shriving laughter.

Allen Klein (1989) points out how "several studies have revealed that many nationally known comedians experienced intense isolation, depression, suffering, or loss in their childhood" (p. 5). However, rather than seeing this as evidence of a causal connection between trauma and comedy, Klein deduces naively that, for these fledgling comedians, "kidding around about their losses and difficulties was a way of gaining power over them" (p. 5).

Legman (1975) presents, however, the opposite case. He asserts that the compulsive joke-teller—particularly the public one—"is only attempting to reassure himself on the subject of his most desperate fears, whistling under his rictus-mask in the darkened parts of his own soul that nauseate and frighten him the most" (p. 19). This is particularly true, according to Legman, of those who feel compelled to provoke laughter in others—joke tellers whose jokes are essentially both a compulsive confession and an evasion of the moral judgment that they deserve and yet desperately fear. This compulsion, according to Legman, explains why so many of Lenny Bruce's routines seemed so full of "painful enthusiasm, almost hysteria" (p. 33). But, as Legman reminds us, most public joke-tellers are not as successful as Bruce was: "Most of them and most of their 'acts' fail, and their little hour on the stage is mercifully brief" (p. 40).

If, as Legman suggests, a person's favorite joke has much to teach us about that person's particular neuroses and anxieties, the same may also be true of the styles of comedy that are the "favorites" of a particular nation or era. The popularity of a certain comedian may reflect the characteristic social problems of a particular cultural group or time. For example, the willingness to mock homosexuality, coupled with the inability to deal with it on a serious level, is symptomatic of profound repression and is highly typical of British comedy. British males of a certain generation, who have been subjected to a particularly sadistic kind of single-sex schooling, are most clearly controlled by the taboo against homosexuality and thus are particularly responsive to its verbal flouting. At a deeper level is the association between homosexuality and the anal. The essence of the anal character, according to Legman (1975), is not only its famous compulsiveness but also its social-sadistic desire to control, especially other people (p. 181)—hence, perhaps, the popularity of anal humor among the British, notorious for their colonial expansions and assumed social superiority.[2]

In the United States, unlike in Britain, many of the best known vaudeville comedians worked in teams, in the style of the Marx Brothers and the Three Stooges. In the heyday of the Borscht Belt, comic pairs became especially popular, for instance, George Burns and Gracie Allen, Carl Reiner and Mel Brooks, the Smothers Brothers, and other canonical clowns. The humor of many of these early comics revolved around banter on social and cultural themes, especially marriage, the family, the relationship between the sexes, and other areas of contemporary sexual and psychological anxiety. Significantly, the relationship between the double act and its audience is similar to that among the joke teller, the joke receiver, and the implied (usually female) third party, and to that among the lover, the adulterous wife, and the cuckolded husband. Both members of the double act compete for the love of their triangulated audience. If their intentions are competitive, nevertheless, their rivalry always draws them into a shared entanglement.

The phenomenally successful pairing of Dean Martin and Jerry Lewis is a good example of how the popularity of a particular stand-up comedian, or pair, relates to contemporary anxieties and neuroses. Most critics attributed the act's success to some aspect of the combination of what Lewis once memorably referred to as "the handsome man and his mon-

---

[2] Legman (1975) explains how the anal element is characterized in culture by looking at the *other side* (or back side) of everything, as in spoonerisms. He characterizes people who like spoonerisms and who like working out their permutations as particularly anal, as are people who "accidentally" fall into them in a habitual way. Apparently such a habit is very common when one is tired, as are erroneous right-and-left gestures, opening things instead of closing them—all gestures that are apparently full of anal and scatological elements (p. 181). For Legman, it is scatology that comes closest to the etymological definition of "obscene": "that which is exceptionally and unexpectedly *brought upon the scene*, into public view. This is particularly evident in the target-area of sexuality (in our dimly remembered quadruped pre-history), as well as the evident exit-point of the feces" (pp. 843–844).

key." In other words, the appeal of Martin and Lewis was not a result of their closeness and cohesion, but of the differences between them: Martin's suave *savoir faire*, and Lewis's ridiculous incompetence. According to film critic Andrew Sarris (1968), "Martin and Lewis at their best . . . had a marvelous tension between them. The great thing about them was their incomparable incompatibility, the persistent sexual hostility" (pp. 142–143).

Critic Robert Kass (1953) had a rather different explanation for the enormous appeal of Martin and Lewis. He suggested that their popularity was related to the fact that, unlike the work of more sophisticated comic acts of the time, their humor had absolutely no relevance to contemporary social or political issues. And since Martin and Lewis were so popular, Kass, fearing that Lewis's "monkey" was a sort of mirror that reflected the social and cultural tendencies of the time, concluded that audiences in the early 1950s were in the mood for facile slapstick, the lowest common denominator of comedy. "We have turned into what Meredith termed 'hypergelasts,'" wrote Kass, "excessive laughers or Bacchanalians, giddy spectators who roar at anything that takes our mind from the problems of our time" (p. 121). Particularly disturbing, according to Kass, was the nihilism of Lewis's humor, its intellectual emptiness: "As for the emasculated, almost homosexual quality of some of Lewis's gags and inflections, they are profoundly anti-human and anti-life, and the response to them is not unalarming. . . . Let us hope there is little of ourselves in the prancing imbeciles and mincing homosexuals he imitates" (p. 122).[3]

---

[3] In two of his films, Jerry Lewis plays the part of a disgruntled clown. In *The Family Jewels* (1965), he plays seven different characters, one of whom is a bitter, dysfunctional clown called Uncle Everett Peyton, who set the standard of hate by which all other evil clowns must subsequently be judged. In *Hardly Working* (1973), Lewis plays an ex-clown who, after failing at several lousy jobs, takes a job with the post office, that last rung on the Federal Government's civil service ladder. Like many other postal workers, even those without the burden of having been professional clowns, Lewis breaks down and, instead of "going postal" in a fast-food outlet, does something even more frightening: he decides to deliver the mail in full clown makeup and regalia. It is perhaps no coincidence that clowns and postal workers alike have come to be closely associated with random violence and groundless evil.

While Martin always remained calm and suave, Lewis placed particular emphasis on his out-of-control physical body. Martin was stable and organized; chaos manifested itself in Lewis's physical body in disarray. Significantly, the 1950s was famously a period of social consensus and conformity, and yet it was also, not coincidentally, a time that saw the emergence of many subversive cultural productions, including beat writing and rock and roll music. The appearance of so many radical cultural forms during an era notorious for its social conservatism indicates that there were perceptible public doubts over whether this kind of mass consensus was really healthy. This skepticism may have been one of the reasons for the enormous appeal of the pairing of a calm crooner and a jumbled fool.

The late 1950s saw the death of the comedy team, and throughout the 1960s most of the best known American stand-up comedians were Jewish heterosexual men, such as Lenny Bruce, Mort Sahl, Robert Klein, Sam Levenson, Jack Benny, and Henny Youngman. John Limon (2000) relates this phenomenon to the rebuilding of America on the suburban model: "Freud's joke theory, which centers on the covering up of laughter's sources in aggression and sex, has . . . the merit of elucidating the suburban moment of American comedy and culture, if suburbs grew on the energy of the same concealments" (p. 3).

Even today, stand-up tends to be a world of male heterosexual machismo. There are very few openly homosexual men in stand-up comedy, which is interesting considering the large numbers of gay men involved in other areas of public performance, such as music and the theater. Moreover, until recently, female stand-up comedians were rare, and even today, most of them provoke laughs by mocking their unfeminine looks and habits. Phyllis Diller jokes about her age and appearance; Joan Rivers ridicules her cosmetic surgery; and Roseanne Barr makes fun of her weight and "white trash" background. It also seems no coincidence that so many female stand-up comics identify themselves as either bisexual (Sandra Bernhard), lesbian (Ellen Degeneres), or asexual (Paula Poundstone). Thrown into conflict with the social codifications of gender and sexuality, the body and identity, class and ethnicity, the stand-up comic inspires a disorderly rewriting of normative protocols.

On a similar note, Limon observes that one of the most distinctive features of stand-up comedy is "the appearance of phallicism" implicit in the performer's erect posture in front of a rigid microphone stand (p. 117). In fact, technologically, the microphone stand is an anachronism; wireless mikes have been used for many years in other kinds of stage performances, including theater, opera, and recitals. Moreover, stand-up comics in countries like France and Italy, where hand gestures are an important part of the language, always use clip-on mikes. But it is difficult to imagine how any stand-up comedian in America today would get by without dependence on this familiar, phallic prop.

Stand-up is a cruel, capricious, and self-centered business. The desire to make people laugh is partly, of course, an aggressive and sadistic wish. Essentially, the joke-teller is using the form of stand-up comedy in order to exteriorize unpleasant truths and experiences, and the joke is a means by which he or she can, as Freud (1905) explained, slough off anxiety on to the listener/victims. By making others laugh, comedians exhibit both their own strength, and the weakness of their audience, which is reduced to apparent helplessness and is thereby no longer threatening.

In fact, stand-up comedy differs from other forms of comedy because it is uniquely audience dependent. Even when televised or played on the radio, stand-up always depends on the presence of a "live" audience (even if its presence is signaled by the eerie canned laughter of dead people)—just as, according to Freud (1905), an untransmitted joke is not, structurally, a joke (p. 431). Thus, the success of the stand-up comedian relies solely and exclusively on the amount of audience laughter he or she can provoke. In other words, the ultimate aim of stand-up comedy is constant, unanimous, uninterrupted laughter. Like extreme pain and sexual abandon, belly laughter obliterates identity; in the deepest moments of laughter, the ego is subsumed by the body's physical convulsions. And when the whole audience laughs, each individual is incorporated into a great mass of hooting, shrieking, roaring bodies. For a fleeting moment, cultural and bodily categories are almost eradicated, as individual members of the audience are fused into a grotesque image of one dense, self-devouring body, with multiple laughing heads yapping all at once like Cerberus.

This, at least, is the ultimate aim of the stand-up comic: an audience that is all body. Once individuality has been neutralized, so has the individual capacity to sit in judgment. An audience that has been weakened and disabled by laughter is an audience that has been made impotent—infantilized even—and thus rendered incapable of disapproval. Most comedians, however, even the very successful ones, are unable to achieve this mass laughter, at least, for more than a few seconds at a time, and so their routine is galvanized by a constant fear that the audience, sitting in paternal judgment, will withhold approbation and offer only the terrible thumbs-down of hollow silence.

And, yet, as I discussed in chapter 3, silence may be in some ways a healthier response to comedy than laughter, since the kind of mass laughter that greets the stand-up comic is often an index of repression and neurosis. As Limon (2000) points out, what is "stood up" in stand-up comedy is abjection (p. 4)—stand-up makes vertical what is normally horizontal, makes conscious what is normally unconscious. In fact, traditional stand-up comedy, as it developed in the back rooms of clubs and bars, was highly offensive and profane, full of racism and misogyny. Common characters included lazy blacks and money-grubbing Jews, limp-wristed queens and nagging wives. When I was growing up, the most popular British stand-up comics had risen to fame in the working men's clubs of northern England—fat, chain-smoking bigots like Bernard Manning and Roy "Chubby" Brown—whose routines consisted of jokes about "wogs," "pakis," "chinks," "birds," and their own sexual frustrations and failures.

That kind of comedy is "abject" in the way Julia Kristeva (1982) uses the term. To Kristeva, abjection refers to a psychic "worrying" of oneself, an attempt to get rid of those aspects of oneself that seem frightening and alien—things like blood, urine, semen, feces, fat, nails, and other kinds of bodily detritus. One of the ways in which we react to abjection, according to Kristeva, is with horror. Another is with laughter. As Kristeva puts it, "Laughter bursts out, facing abjection, and always originating in the same source, of which Freud had caught a glimpse: the gushing forth of the unconscious, the repressed, suppressed pleasure, be it sex or death" (pp. 205–206).

But "abjection" also has the sense of abasement or groveling prostration, and Limon (2000) points out that this is not incompatible with the way in which Kristeva (1982) uses the term. "When you feel abject," writes Limon (2000), "you feel as if there were something miring your life, some skin that cannot be sloughed, some role (because 'abject' always, in a way, describes how you *act*) that has become your only character. Abjection is self-typecasting" (p. 4). What makes us laugh, in other words, is the shame that our proxy, the stand-up comic, feels about his or her very existence.

Generally playing the part of an outsider or social misfit, the stand-up comedian presents a spectacle of otherness by serving as a conduit for energies that are marginal, nonnormative, or antisocial. The resulting conflicts between the comedian and the (social) world may also be played out through intrapsychic divisions, with the comedian playing the role of an eccentric individual who, knowingly or unknowingly, disrupts conventional norms of behavior, thought, and identity. This may be why the personae of most successful stand-up comedians are either awkward and submissive (Ellen Degeneres, Woody Allen, Paula Poundstone, Emo Philips) or the opposite, aggressive and arrogant, in an obvious attempt to deny or cover up the insecurity (Richard Pryor, Robin Williams, Eddie Murphy, Andrew Dice Clay).

If those people who fancy themselves as comedians were not aggrieved and in pain in the first place, chances are that they would never have felt called upon to comment humorously on the passing scene. Legman (1975) has some incisive comments about those who feel compelled to tell jokes on a regular basis, especially when such characters have, as Legman puts it, "a need to 'do their thing' aggressively and publicly," and have "found a protective cover for their neurosis" in forms like popular entertainment (p. 39).

Perhaps this is why so many comedians end up getting thoroughly sick of their comic personae. For example, stand-up comedian Rick Reynolds (1992) confesses to experiencing a sudden moment of insight when a fellow plane passenger asked him what he did for a living, and he felt compelled to lie: "I was suddenly ashamed of being a stand-up comedian. Suddenly stand-up comedy seemed kind of dirty to me" (p. 20). Later, Reynolds reveals that he never enjoyed being a stand-up comic, not even at the beginning: "There was always an inherent deception in the delivery of my material that seemed almost sinister. An actor gets up on stage every night and pretends to be somebody else. I got up on stage every night and pretended to be myself" (p. 22).

Reynolds's autobiography is not unusual; memoirs by comedians more often than not describe lives of anguish and abuse. Another stand-up comic who has gone public with his own self-hatred is Richard Lewis (2002). His memoir describes what Lewis refers to as his "insidious . . . never-ending, nauseating, daunting need always to write and perform" (p. xiv). "I thought if I could make light of how much I hated myself I would magically mend" (p. 48), Lewis reveals, referring to the domain of stand-up comedy as a world of "jealousy, greed, guilt-tripping, egomania, thievery, lying, manipulation, bullshit, sleaze, and intercourse without soul" (p. 51). He describes "the decades of humiliating myself on stage for laughs" as no more than "just a dirty habit" (p. xiv), fraught with the constant anxiety that "maybe I was wasting my life, and that my obsession with becoming a successful comedian would turn into one big joke, with me as *the punch line from hell*" (p. 86).

In the last 20 years stand-up comedy has remained a growing force in popular entertainment, particularly since the advent of the cable channel Comedy Central, which first went on air in 1995 and which devotes much of its daytime programming to stand-up. The kind of stand-up comedy that is shown on television, however, seems increasingly anodyne. The racist and misogynistic routines of comedians like Richard Pryor and Andrew Dice Clay have been replaced by other kinds of comedy, such as humor that deals in tiny observations about daily life—a form perfected by stand-ups like Jerry Seinfeld and Ellen Degeneres—or comedy based on social or political issues, the kind of thing done very well by Janeane Garofolo and Dennis Leary. And then there are comedians like Richard Lewis and Kathy Griffin, who simply like to poke fun at their own inadequacies.

Stand-up today is so much less offensive than it used to be partly because success today, for stand-up comedians, depends on their ability to cross over into mainstream television, and, beyond that, into other, more anodyne forms, such as the sitcom and the talk show. Of course, early stand-up comedians also graduated into radio and television sitcoms. But these were mainly regarded as sidelines, and stand-up comedy remained the bread-and-butter of most performers' lives, including successful television personalities like Jackie Gleason and Sid Caesar. Today, however, no really successful stand-up comic remains a stand-up comic for long, as is evident from the career trajectories of former stand-ups like Roseanne Barr, Jerry Seinfeld, Whoopi Goldberg, Eddie Murphy, and Robin Williams. The more violent and offensive kinds of comedians may still ply their routines in bars and nightclubs, at roasts, and at private parties, but there is clearly no room in the mainstream for explicit abjection.

While some may applaud this "cleaning up" of comedy, it is important to remember that the stand-up comic has traditionally functioned as a cultural scapegoat, manifesting our deep-seated antisocial urge to admit what we truly feel. Deprived of our traditional court fools, with their sacrosanct ability to tell the truth, the abjection turns inward, leaving us to wonder, Where will this rage and hatred manifest itself now that the jester has been sent into exile?

CHAPTER *6*

Against Humor Therapy

At the Harborplace Marriott Hotel in Baltimore, Maryland, the vogue is for motley: striped pants and harlequin ties for the gents, oversized, fruit-shaped jewelry and animal-print sweaters for the ladies. Clowns chat seriously with psychiatrists; lawyers brush shoulders with spiritual healers; teachers exchange cards with businessmen and therapists. In one booth, an "empath and visionary" offers to photograph and analyze your aura for 15 bucks. At another, a "Humor Consultant, Speaker, EntertRainer" offers to sell you Groucho Glasses and Tickling Sticks at less than market price. Welcome to the 2002 Annual Conference of the Association for Applied and Therapeutic Humor.

Audiences at the panels are relaxed. People are knitting, eating potato salad, chatting with each other, and interrupting the speakers with jokes and personal anecdotes. Presenters are occasionally drowned out by the raucous laughter and honking of hooters coming from neighboring conference rooms. A number of participants have chosen to sport appropriately "humorous" attire—pink fright wigs, red noses, striped suspenders, and baseball caps with propellers on top. In the halls music is playing, and people laugh and chat in front of stalls where clown costumes, props, and books are sold. Comic "doctors" sporting joke "stethoscopes" mingle with people wearing "funny" teeth and musicians playing tom-tom drums and guitars. A number of women wear garlands of paper flowers around their heads, like refugees from a pagan ritual; others carry cuddly toy mascots. People refer to the plenary speakers by their first names,

Patty, Allen, and Sandy, as though they were everyone's special friends.

As might be imagined, a number of the speakers at the conference dealt with the importance of humor in response to the events of September 11, 2001. The meetings included a Free Public Symposium titled "Tragedy, Laughter, and Survival of the Spirit," for which a panel of experts convened to discuss "how humor and laughter can help people cope with and recover from disaster, war and tragedy." One of the speakers was "jollytologist" Allen Klein (1989, 1998), perhaps today's most influential secular exponent of humor therapy. Klein, an exponent of "ho-holistic therapy," gave a talk on "How Can You Laugh at a Time Like This?" in which he claimed that "humor took five days to return" after September 11. He gave examples of jokes and cartoons on subjects like the anthrax scare and the whereabouts of Osama Bin Laden.

Like most of the presenters at the convention, Klein offered no more than a series of personal anecdotes testifying to the tired truism that people usually manage to keep their sense of humor even in the most difficult of times. Other speakers, however, had even less to say. In a serious, sparsely attended presentation on "Humor During Wartime—Lessons for Living," self-styled "humorist" George Scherer made the startling claim that "nonmirthful laughter is better than no laughter at all," and the Afghani citizens who were seen dancing in the streets after the destruction of the World Trade Center should be applauded, because "at least they got some humor out of it." Scherer advised his audience to volunteer to help in times of crisis, to buy American flags, to maintain a sense of humor "for America," and to keep up their "network of humor." "A smile is better than a frown," he concluded.

In a presentation titled "Chuckles in Chaos, Laughter in Disaster," registered nurse Sandy Ritz reminded us that "Evil is live spelled backwards" and displayed numerous slides, comic strips, puns, props, and masks to facilitate a group discussion of "happiness," "sadness," and the "new normal." "Our souls have been injured," concluded Ms. Ritz. "We're humor impaired; we need humor rehab. Laughter clears the pipes, and the feeling can come through again." And in a presentation called "Laughter in Hell: Humor and the Holocaust," author Steve Lipman recounted a number of anecdotal tales of people's experiences of humor during the holocaust as "strategies for hoping and coping."

Another panel, by an educator known as "Hubba Jubba," was titled simply "Laughter Builds Enthusiasm." Hubba Jubba's aim is to help people to stop thinking about their problems through the use of humor. The seminar room in which he gave his presentation was covered in posters and pictures, mainly colorful paper plates with smiles on them. He asked his audience to make eye contact and encouraged them to sing along to a humorous song and to give their "heartiest and most healthy laugh." His mottos include "There's magic in our laffter," "Enthusiasm is one of the greatest values we can build within ourselves," and "Enthusiasm equals body gestures of extravagance." He demonstrated different handshakes and encouraged his audience to shake hands with one another and to "get to know a stranger."

Between bouts of booming, apparently unmotivated laughter, Hubba Jubba explained that he used to be a physical education instructor until he got too old and put on too much weight. Now, it seems, nothing is left but his enthusiasm, isolated, free floating, and detached, like the smile of the Cheshire Cat.

The Association for Applied and Therapeutic Humor was established in 1988 to promote the "healing power of laughter and humor.[1] The AATH is interdisciplinary in nature, but most advocates of humor therapy approach the subject from a psychodynamic or a rational-emotional perspective. The organization was founded partly in response to the enormous increase in interest in the use of humor in therapeutic situations since the 1980s.

But it is not only in the West that people have come to believe in the "healing powers of humor." There are over 200 "Laughter Clubs" in India, many implemented as part of the corporate routine in offices and factories. These Laughter Clubs promote the practice of "Laughter Yoga," developed by Dr. Madan Kataria. It is a type of group meditation that involves breathing and stretching exercises followed by a session of group laughter. Its aim is to increase oxygen levels in the body, release endorphins, increase self-confidence, and develop leadership qualities among participants. According to Dr. Kataria,

---

[1] See home page of the American Association for Therapeutic Humor (www.aath.org).

All the Laughter Club members try to identify and remove the negative factors like guilt, anger, fear, jealousy and ego, which stop us from laughing. They cultivate the spirit of laughter by following ways and means of sensible living, like paying compliments, the art of forgiveness, and understanding human relationships.[2]

According to the AATH, the 1990s produced "scientific evidence" to support the anecdotal claims from previous decades that laughter is good medicine, mainly in its capacity to "release endorphins" and "distract the patient from pain." Apparently, more and more hospitals everywhere are enabling their patients to benefit from such powers. In one hospital in North Carolina, a "laughmobile" rolls from room to room. At another hospital, the El Camino in Mountain View, California, patients can tune in to a closed-circuit "laughter channel" launched by pathologist Josh Sickel, who believes that humor should be part of every medical treatment protocol. There is a Laughter Therapy organization in Studio City, and another in Santa Barbara. Similar groups include the Health and Humor Association in Norfolk, Virginia, and the Laughter Remedy Institution in Montclair, New Jersey. Most disturbing of all, perhaps, are the sinister goings-on at the Gesundheit Institute in Hillsboro, West Virginia, the famous "silly hospital" trumpeted obnoxiously in the gut-churning Robin Williams vehicle, *Patch Adams*.

There is an enormous literature on the relationship between humor and psychotherapy, most of it written by practicing humor therapists, and most of it having nothing to do with the principles of psychoanalysis as established by Freud and others. Given most people's *desire* for a connection between health and humor, and given the tendency of the popular media to oversimplify and extrapolate any exciting and optimistic new idea, it is perhaps inevitable that the associations between humor and physical well-being have been endlessly exaggerated.

Freud (1927) wrote about the psychological place of humor in gratifying sexual and aggressive drives, but it is psychoanalyst Martin Grotjahn (1949) who is credited with first publicly advocating the use of humor in psychotherapy. Grotjahn's work was not followed up at the time, how-

---

[2] See www.latterklub.dk.

ever, and there was little else written about the therapeutic use of humor until the 1980s, when Freud's work was becoming increasingly "Americanized" and diluted into various other kinds of therapeutic and counseling techniques. The resultant popular, simplified version of Freudian psychoanalysis has appropriated certain very accessible concepts that seem to fit easily into the contemporary therapeutic mindset—concepts like repression, projection, and denial—while neglecting ideas that fit this climate less comfortably, such as the important connections Freud outlined between humor and hostility.

The modern "humor therapy" movement has some of its roots in Norman Cousins's (1979) well-known book, *Anatomy of an Illness as Perceived by the Patient.* In 1964, Cousins, then editor of the *Saturday Review*, an influential intellectual magazine, suddenly became ill with a serious and painful collagen disease after returning home from a visit to Moscow. After doctors proved unable to find a cure for his high fever and severe pain, Cousins decided to leave the hospital and try a unique approach to his medical treatment.

Part of the theory behind Cousins's unorthodox regimen was the speculation that, since emotions like frustration and suppressed rage are believed to have negative effects on body chemistry, positive emotions should have the opposite effect. Consequently, Cousins left the hospital, checked into a hotel, and spent his time watching some of his favorite Marx Brothers movies and Candid Camera episodes until the pain eventually disappeared. This part of his treatment led to the development of the enduring myth, still perpetuated in the popular press, that Cousins "cured himself with laughter"—an assumption often backed up by a much-quoted statement from *Anatomy of an Illness:* "I made the joyous discovery that ten minutes of genuine belly laughter had an anaesthetic effect and would give me at least two hours of pain-free sleep" (p. 39).

Cousins's book was, of course, enormously popular and encouraged the widespread assumption that laughter is beneficial to one's physical and psychological well-being. Cousins's remission, however, as he readily admitted, was due mainly to the administration of enormous doses of ascorbic acid and other medical procedures, and not necessarily related to laughter. The case is often cited as though Cousins were a smart layman who, disappointed with his progress in the hospital, decided to take matters into his own hands and managed to cure himself through regular bouts of belly-laughs. What is perhaps less well known about Cousins is that at the time of his illness, as well as being editor of the *Saturday Review*, he was an expert on health and fitness and later became a senior lecturer and patients' advocate at UCLA's School of Medicine.

Cousins (1979) claims that there is a significant connection between health and humor, but he provides no empirical support for this assertion, and there is still no scientific evidence to support his many claims about the physiological benefits of laughter. *Anatomy of an Illness* remains very popular even today, despite Cousins's appalling taste in comedy and his failure to engage at even a basic level with the imaginative life of the sick. Another of the problems of Cousins's work—and with many subsequent writings on the subject—is that he tends to use the words *humor* and *laughter* interchangeably, whereas these are, of course, qualitatively different phenomena. As Legman (1975) explains, laughter can be used to humiliate, provoke and disgust; moreover, most of the human laughter that takes place during ordinary social intercourse serves simply to modify the behavior of others by shaping the emotional tone of a conversation and is not necessarily associated with what we have come to call "humor."

There has been much speculation, but no empirical support, for the claim that laughter triggers the release of endorphins. Some researchers have claimed that laughter can help stimulate the production of boosters to our immune system, which may be true, but so can all activities that stimulate the heart rate, including, for that matter, acts of violence and aggression. Nevertheless, there seems to be a deep-seated need to believe in the power of humor and to believe that we are instinctively drawn to it because it is somehow good for the soul, and not because it distracts us from those things we are unable to face. As Diana Mahony (2000), points out, it is understandably tempting to believe that any program or activity that we engage in by choice is beneficial to our well-being. Engaging in humor after a loss certainly helps to encourage social relations, bonding with others, verbalization, and so on—but, then, so does the grieving process. It is obviously true that laughter might make us feel better for a while by distracting us from our pain, but so do many other things: meditation, prayer, listening to music, petting animals, reading, sneezing, masturbating, and even, for that matter, having a good old-fashioned cry.

Anatomy of an Illness was hastily followed by a spate of self-help-through-humor manuals, the introduction of humor into counseling programs and workshops, and a plague of magazine and journal articles on the importance of humor in social relationships, especially in therapy. Since the 1980s, there has been an enormous increase in interest in the use of humor in therapeutic situations, resulting in the publication of numerous newsletters and magazine articles on the subject and the establishment of all kinds of different meeting groups and conferences. The interest in therapeutic humor is growing stronger every year, even though most of the strident claims made about its salubrious benefits remain essentially untested empirically, and despite continuing controversy regarding the use of humor in therapeutic situations. Even seasoned advocates of such techniques agree there has been little empirical study to demonstrate the specific therapeutic benefits of humor and laughter (see, e.g., Ventis, Higbee, and Murdock, 2001).

Moreover, discussions of humor therapy, even among its practitioners, are usually couched in a vocabulary that is far more vague and circumstantial than most discussions of therapeutic procedures; by way of example, one discussion, "Which Humor for Doctors?" (1998), describes the ultimate goal of such therapy as being "to release the joy of the hidden fun child." Conveniently, such discussions generally ignore the connections, expounded at length by Freud (1927) and Legman (1968), between humor and sadistic, aggressive impulses, and the use of humor to obscure hostility and frustration.

Despite all the talk of the benefits of therapeutic humor, it is very difficult to find examples of how such therapy functions in a practical situation. Indeed, the AATH's official definition of therapeutic humor includes

any intervention that promotes health and wellness by stimulating a playful discovery, expression or appreciation of the absurdity or incongruity of life's situation. This intervention may enhance

health or be used as a complementary treatment of illness to facilitate healing or coping, whether physical, emotional, cognitive,
social or spiritual.[3]

According to psychologist Louis Franzini (2001), "interventions" may
include such activities as reciting jokes or riddles, pointing out absurdi-
ties or puns, drawing attention to examples of illogical reasoning, exag-
gerating to the extreme, making statements of self-deprecation, repeating
an amusing punchline, and making comical observations about current
social and environmental events (pp. 170–197).

Some practitioners, however, are more specific about the techniques
they use in humor therapy. The best known humor therapists seem to
have developed their own individual therapeutic "styles," in which humor
is inserted into the therapeutic process in various ways. These include
Walter O'Connell's (1987) "natural high" theory, Richard Driscoll's (1987)
use of humor in pragmatic psychotherapy, W. Larry Ventis's (1987) work
with humor and laughter in behavior therapy, and Frank Farrelly and
Michael Lynch's (1987) use of humor in "provocative" therapy.[4] Many of
these humor therapists are self-styled "guru"-types, some of whom have
developed (and copyrighted) their own variants of the use of humor in
the therapeutic context (with video and audio tapes available for sale, at
a reduced price for patients).

A typical example is clinical psychologist Albert Ellis's (1984, 1987)
Rational Emotive Therapy, which involves applying (copyrighted) humorous lyrics to well-known show tunes. Ellis, a therapist who is outspoken
in his advocacy of the use of humor during therapy, regularly leads his
clients in "group singing of familiar tunes whose silly lyrics have been
modified" (p. 6). Such techniques encourage the suspicion that these
kinds of therapy may, in fact, be ways for the conscious or unconscious
problems of the *therapists* to find a socially acceptable (and financially
profitable) avenue of expression and petcock of release.

---

[3] See www.humormatters.com/definiti.htm.

[4] Farrelly is quite candid about the origins of Provocative Therapy—he came
upon the technique during a session with a female patient in which the fly of his
trousers became inadvertently unzipped as he and his patient discussed her sexual infidelity toward her husband.

Psychiatrist and holocaust survivor Viktor E. Frankl (1946) describes some more subtle and thoughtful work involving humor and "paradoxical intention," in which the therapist prescribes the symptom in a massive dose—the patient is instructed to surrender to what he or she has been fighting. Similarly, Gordon W. Allport (1937) also highlights the role of humor in promoting "self-objectification." It may certainly be true, as Allport points out, that in particular therapeutic situations joking may be a helpful device in promoting social skills, reducing tension, encouraging cohesiveness, and giving some kind of insight into interpersonal dynamics. Unfortunately, however, much of this potentially interesting work is marred by an unquestioning assumption about what humor *is*, as well as unexamined clichés about the "healing force" of humor and laughter in general.

Despite the extent of the literature advocating the use of humor in therapy, it is very difficult to find advice about actual techniques to use and explanations of why humor is so important in the therapeutic situation. Also rare are articles that recommend specific humor training for practitioners.[5] Some humor therapists offer classes and workshops in developing a sense of humor, didactic humor-training seminars featuring discussions, readings, role playing, and so on. Yet at the same time, it seems almost universally accepted that the undefined, elusive "sense of humor" is something you either have or don't have; it's not something that can ever be "forced." In fact, tactics suggested for those who want to bring more humor into the therapeutic relationship seem to be actions that any intelligent, sensible person would use anyway without thinking twice. They include the kinds of jokes, anecdotes, and asides that most people already incorporate into their conversation quite naturally through certain vocal and behavioral gestures. By definition they are spontaneous, freely moving, and rather difficult to anticipate or describe. These kinds of gestures are subtle, fleeting, and evanescent and significantly different from defensive jolliness or jokiness.

Surely the majority of thoughtful, sophisticated therapists, like most other people, tend to use humor implicitly—even unconsciously—with-

---

[5] Important exceptions include the work of Sultanoff (1994) and Thompson (1990).

out seeking further elaborations or theoretical justification for their humorous "interventions." Surely most intelligent therapists know how to use humor instinctively, without having to make it explicitly the cornerstone of their therapeutic work, or develop new theories about it, or offer workshops to explain and promote its use. Most people use, share, and generate humor in their daily lives all the time, without giving it a second thought. Most of the workshops, in fact, sound like little more than seminars in how to be a more interesting person. Is it really necessary to take a class in "behavioral environmental management theory" in order to learn how to make "an explicitly humor-oriented consulting room with funny posters, quotes or cartoons"? Do therapists really have to take seminars in "clinical humor" or "humor immersion training," as recommended by W. A. Salameh (1994), for example, to be able "to use their own personal history and their own physical characteristics to identify funniness in their lives" (p. 5)?

Perhaps the most obvious omission in all these many different kinds of "humor therapy" is that nowhere do any of its practitioners seem to ask what "humor" actually *is*. Virtually every advocate of humor therapy takes for granted, first, that we all know and agree what constitutes humor and, second, that humor is without question an obvious force for good. Any implication that much of what passes for "humor" might be regressive, and even evidence of neurosis, is immediately laughed off. Research on humor is generally approached as if humor were an external, reliably measurable "thing" readily available for unequivocal classification.

As Legman has helped us to understand, however, it is difficult to think of any word in the English language harder to define than "humor." Theories "explaining" the nature of humor seem to be innumerable, but none seems to come close to capturing the concept in its slippery sum. Most of these "explanations" seem to regard humor as an external "something," a discrete phenomenon that can be trapped, caged, and prodded like a rare animal, rather than an intervening variable. One of the most glaring weaknesses of psychological research on this subject is the enormous discrepancy between the theoretical implications of the concept of humor and the kinds of examples chosen to measure the concept. "What is striking about the literature on laughter and health," writes humor scholar Jeffrey H. Goldstein (1987), "is how far our convictions exceed our knowledge" (p. 15).

I should perhaps point out here that "humor therapy" is most often used as a form of psychological counseling and has no connection with any branch of psychoanalysis. Nor should it be confused with the use of play in therapy, which has a long and important history in traditional forms of psychoanalysis, and not only with children. Philosopher Friedrich Schiller (1795) regarded play as the manifestation of an integrating function that is the vehicle of symbolization, and many contemporary analysts are strongly in favor of the use of play in helping adults and children alike to facilitate integration and to understand the use of symbols. To those who advocate its use, especially Piaget (1951), Huizinga (1994), Solnit (1987), Moran (1987), Carpy (1989), and Klauber (1986), playfulness in therapy can be of great value in the establishment, maintenance, and advancement of a viable analytic process and can also serve as a distinct measure of analytic achievement.

Within the psychoanalytic tradition, psychotherapy as play, or as the acquisition of the capacity to play, is rooted in the writings of the British object relations theorist D. W. Winnicott, mainly in his seminal *Playing and Reality* (1971). Winnicott regards playing as essential to the analytic experience and as a process that can be both thrilling and frightening in its use of such precarious elements as role-playing and paradoxes. According to Winnicott, the skilful analyst learns how to use play instinctively in therapy—precisely when to intervene; when to pick up a cue; when to deal in the irrational, the unknown, the ambiguous, and the unpredictable.

This is a process that Cynthia Rose (2002) refers to as "catching the ball." The best contemporary account of this kind of creative play in therapy is contained in Jean Sanville's (1991) wise and thoughtful book, *The Playground of Psychoanalytic Therapy*. As Sanville's account of her techniques makes clear, this sort of play is a subtle and partly instinctual process and has nothing to do with the premeditated and often ponderous interventions of the "humor therapist."

The current popularity of "humor therapy" is intricately bound up with the fact that human laughter is almost always believed to be a manifestation of, or an accompaniment to, health and humor. In human beings, laughter is commonly regarded unidimensionally, as taking only one form, which is consistently positive and life affirming. However simplistic this viewpoint may be, it is far more popular and widely accepted than Freud's (1905) suggestion that there might be a neurotic component to laughter. The "humor" and "laughter" therapy movements are born of the debatable therapeutic assumption that self-assertion and self-expression are innately satisfying activities that promote relaxation and allow people to discuss their feelings more readily. In point of fact, "humor therapy" is premised on the denial of mental disorder, even of underlying notions of psychological conflict and developmental deficit per se—which are not laughing matters.

For example, "jollytologist" Allen Klein—the leading light of the "humor therapy" movement and one of the keynote speakers at the 2002 AATH conference—focuses not on the importance of humor in the therapeutic situation, but on the ways in which "ordinary people" like us can use humor to "improve our quality of life." Klein, not a therapist or psychologist but an after-dinner speaker, believes that, if we lack humor, it is a sign that our lives are out of balance, which can lead to both physical and mental illness. Klein (1998) argues that people who are depressed and suicidal have lost all perspective in their lives. "They take themselves and the world so seriously and get so caught up in their dilemmas," he writes, "that they cannot see any way out" (p. 16).

Similarly, much of what is written under the guise of "humor therapy" is little more than a batch of elementary platitudes encouraging people to develop a positive attitude and look on the bright side. For example, Klein (1989) suggests that we increase the amount of laughter in our lives by telling one joke a week to as many people as we can. "At the end of the week," he promises, "you will know one joke. At the end of the month, four. By the end of the year, you will know 52" (p. 38). Other important elements of Klein's humor-enhancing protocol include surrounding yourself with little cutouts and pictures that make you laugh (his own bulletin board, he reveals, "is filled with cutouts of laughing lips, smile buttons, and clown cards" [p. 80]). Elsewhere, he encourages his readers to "draw a picture or secure a photo of yourself in which you are laughing," and then "keep this picture in a place where you see it often. It is a reminder that you can laugh" (p. 82).

Klein cites the rather disturbing example of psychotherapist Harold Greenwald, who brings humor into his therapy sessions by impersonating his clients, to suggest that, when visiting patients in hospital, we follow Greenwald's example by walking into the room wearing Groucho glasses or a red clown's nose (p. 82). "A pair of Groucho glasses or a rubber chicken strategically placed may be just what you need," he believes (pp. 87–88). Klein advises us to imagine we are accompanied by an inflatable clown who will listen to our problems and show us how to lighten up (p. 84). Much of his work does not get beyond this basic level of advice. Klein himself sounds like a frightening person to know. He explains proudly that he has been known to grab a parking meter and use it as a microphone to state his case to a disagreeing companion; and, when faced with what he believes to be "boring dinner conversation," he likes to drape his dinner napkin over his face, put his glasses on over the napkin, and continue eating his meal that way (p. 148).

By the end of that book, Klein has been reduced to such feeble inanities as quoting "uplifting" song lyrics from *Annie* and drafting senseless apothegms about getting our "maximum requirement of vitamin H each and every day" and seeing the world as our "Laff Lab" (pp. 150–151). When faced with an insurmountable crisis, we are advised to think about how Lucille Ball or Groucho Marx would handle things (p. 104). Finally, Klein recounts some amusing bumper stickers he has seen, suggests that we distract ourselves by watching "situation-comedy television shows" and listening to "comedy records," and reminds us that we live in a "crazy, laughable world" and should all try to take ourselves a little less seriously (pp. 106–108).

Like many other advocates of humor therapy, Klein believes that, until people can laugh at their own tragedies, they have not completely processed their human experience. Laughter, especially in times of trouble, is always regarded as an indication of balance, health, and all-round well being, but the techniques proposed to induce such laughter, as Klein's work testifies, seem disturbingly obvious.

Similarly glib examples of humor therapy techniques are advocated in a peer-reviewed article on the use of humor among addiction counselors by Sharon Tamargo Weaver and C. Nick Wilson (1997). They suggest sticking up children's drawings and funny cartoons on the walls and piping "elevator music" into the waiting room. We are warned that "constant intellectualizing decreases the ability to acknowledge one's playfulness"; and—with no attempt to question or raise the problematics of such notions as "fun" and "humor"—we are reminded that "humor allows us to laugh at ourselves" and that "counselors who have fun at work are more likely to look forward to each work day" (p. 108). Significantly, those therapists who are resistant to humor are often accused of having "issues" with closeness and power. Instead of being seen as seriously concerned about the potentially destructive and retrogressive effects of humor in the therapeutic context, such therapists are usually considered to be overinvested in power dynamics and afraid of the loss of status that would result from putting themselves on the same level as their clients (see, for example, the aptly named Jolley, 1982).

Most people would not question the assumption that humor and laughter have an important role to play in encouraging physical health and supporting well-being. Comedy, especially at the cinema and on television, is automatically associated with uplifting entertainment, lightheartedness, and not taking things too seriously. Most often, laughter is regarded as a moment of joy, perhaps of rebellion, stimulated by a playful discovery, expression, or appreciation of the absurdity or incongruity of life's situations. In Western culture, laughter is so commonly associated with pleasure that to suggest it may sometimes have a neurotic component seems both perverse and misanthropic.

But according to Freud (1905), humor can also be nervous, neurotic, and pathological. It may certainly distract us from our pain and help us put aside our fears, our discomforts, and our concerns about our health, but is this necessarily a positive step? Some patients need to face the sober fact that their illness is not treatable; others need to deal with the approach of their own death or the death of a loved one. It seems neither helpful nor appropriate to make light of such experiences. Humor may serve as a distraction from stress and pain, but is not distraction, after all, just another form of that dreaded therapeutic shibboleth, *denial?*

Interestingly, it is only in the last hundred years or less that public laughter has been widely acceptable in polite society. Throughout many periods in Western culture, laughter was thought to be rude at best, sinful at worst. There are still some therapists who regard chronic joking as an anathema, an impediment to effective treatment; some even regard it as unethical, which makes some sense, because we have all experienced the pain of being mocked, teased, ridiculed, or laughed at. And the cruelty of hostile humor can be greater than that of a direct insult.

Some therapists—especially Brody (1950), Kaplan and Boyd (1965), Searles (1979), Kubie (1971), and Marcus (1990)—have even been brave enough to suggest that humor in a therapeutic context can be damaging and dangerous. It has been claimed, for example, that the inappropriate use of satire can lead to a patient's feeling humiliated or ridiculed, and untimely exaggeration or the telling of a formal joke might create the impression that the therapist is insensitive, uncaring, or excessively self-absorbed. A few therapists, suggesting that humor has no role in the therapeutic situation, are completely opposed to it in the treatment room.

Brody (1950) observed that, in his experience, it was only the most damaged types of personalities (the schizophrenic, schizoid, or compulsive) who smiled or laughed during the analytic sessions. Brody suggested that the analyst may call attention to this laughter, but once this has happened, the patient may well become uneasy, fearing he is being laughed at or is being accused of having laughed at the analyst. According to Brody:

Laughter is a defense best left undisturbed, for the superficial cloud of mirth that cloaks it is all too easily dissipated, leaving a substance of sadness, despair, regret, anger or hatred that may overwhelm the patient. This we found true in nearly every instance where we persisted in attempting to analyze our patients' laughter. In most instances the meaning of the laughter arose from such deep sources of the unconscious and was so far removed from the patient's understanding that it was futile to continue its pursuit [p. 193].

In an important early study of the social functions of humor on an open psychiatric ward, Howard B. Kaplan and Ina H. Boyd (1965) concluded that the humor of psychiatric patients generally dealt with themes that were especially pertinent to their situation—themes like dependency, sex and obscenity, severe mental disorders, and hostility toward staff, "civilians" and other patients. This observation clearly supports Legman's claim that the principal function of humor—and, certainly, the acceptance of things as humorous that are not really humorous at all—is to relieve the accumulated tension created by living in a difficult and painful situation, such as life in a psychiatric institution might create.

According to Searles (1979) and Kubie (1971), patients may sometimes mock even their own symptoms in their efforts to avoid accepting help. To join in the patient's laughter, or to encourage it, may perhaps be to promote humor at the patient's expense; the therapist may fall into a trap unconsciously set by the patient's own neurosis. This is true of patients whose illnesses are physical, as well as those with psychiatric illness. In the therapeutic situation especially, laughter does not necessarily reflect a state of adjustment or physical well-being. It may indicate hostility, self-deprecation, or defensiveness. In group therapy, laughter may be used as a tactic for manipulation, ingratiation, denial, or control.

There seem to be so many ways in which the use of humor in therapy could go horribly wrong that it could easily sidetrack the discussions and lead the patient astray from his or her original path. It may lead to a derailment, a distraction, or an artificial destination. Also, compliant patients may feel compelled to go along with the therapist's jokes so as to ingratiate themselves, and make them feel that their treatment is successful. But even this kind of laughter can be misleading, as in an early example from Searles (1979) in which a psychiatric patient was accustomed to mimicking the various different laughs of the nurses in the hospital.

> Her early laughs were done with such "skill" that I thought her genuinely happy, found her laughs often infectious, and laughed with her. But then, as she went on laughing from time to time, the eeriness of what she was doing grew more and more upon me: it became increasingly clear to me that this woman was momentarily hiding her massive despair by imitating laughs for which she, unlike the original authors, had at the moment no correspondingly genuine wellspring of happiness [p. 48].

No evidence has ever been presented to justify the therapeutic use of humor with paranoid patients, who might very well regard any attempts at humor with suspicion and hostility. The same may also be true of group patients in therapy, where laughter could very easily have a contagious, infectious influence when an anxiety-arousing subject is shared by many of its members. Vargas (1961) eloquently describes a failed attempt to use humor in group therapy: "More and more problems were revealed, and more and more injustices and disturbing conditions were explored and yet each deeper condition was greeted with increasing hilarity" (p. 200).

However, such honest discussions about the damaging potential of humor in psychotherapy are increasingly rare. For obvious reasons, most therapists are very reluctant to publish case studies that depict their own failures. In fact, of all the therapists and counselors who have written about their uses of humor in psychotherapy, only a small handful describe therapeutic failures. Perhaps the most important of these is a highly controversial article by psychiatrist Lawrence Kubie (1971). Kubie claimed that, despite long years of experience in private and hospital psychiatric practices, he was unable to point to a single patient in whose treatment humor proved to be a safe, valuable, and necessary aid. He *did*, however, report that he often picked up traces of patients' delayed, bitter responses to the lighthearted or bantering approach of the therapist. One of his patients had actually been traumatized by "two painful experiences with humorous therapists" (p. 39). Kubie's article has been widely attacked, but never convincingly; of course, it makes disturbing reading, especially to those who like to think of laughter as part of the joyful wonder of human life.

According to Kubie, a patient's humor can often be a way of seducing the therapist out of his therapeutic role and into one of participation in mutual "fun." The use of humor on the part of the therapist, moreover, is often simply a form of arrogant self-display, exhibitionism, or "wooing." Admonishing the therapist to admit that their humor is essentially a form of self-display ("see how bright and witty and amusing and charming and delightful I can be!" [p. 40]), Kubie insists that the use of humor during therapy amounts to a callous misuse of the patient as a captive audience. And when the therapist insists on demonstrating how bright, funny, and appealing he is, the patient suddenly gets trapped in a horrible involuntary "laugh-in," afraid to anger the therapist by not joining in with the joke. "The secret devastation that goes on inside comes to light only much later," claims Kubie (p. 40). He concludes with a piece of advice that Legman would sanction wholeheartedly—a warning to investigate the personal insecurities of those who like to broadcast the benefits of "humor therapy":

> Those who are most violent in their defense of humor in psychotherapy often have faces that are distorted with anger even when they think they are at peace and unobserved. Any lecturer on this topic, particularly if the group is not too large, can spot them in the audience by their chronic expressions of tense resentment. These men do not want to be deprived of their right to use and misuse something that they misterm "humor." . . . Humor has its place in life. Let us keep it there by acknowledging that one place where it has a very limited role, if any, is in psychotherapy [p. 42].

Obviously, the work of Kubie, Brody, and Searles is severely dated, and the kind of talk therapy that forms the basis of traditional psychoanalysis is no longer the primary mode of dealing with the mentally ill. Still, there are many mental health professionals today who would agree with Kubie that humor initiated in any kind of therapeutic situation is usually no more than "bantering in the dark," as Kubie puts it, and humor engaged in by patients can often be a defense against accepting the seriousness of their own problems: "Wit would appear to have little therapeutic impact, and doctors who indulge in it do so for their own amusement or as a defensive mechanism" ("Which Humor for Doctors?" p. 95). Psychotherapists Alan Kazdin (1999) and Bernard Saper (1987), moreover, both agree that the use of humor in therapy can be very dangerous indeed.

Equally persuasive is the work of psychotherapist N. N. Marcus (1990). Marcus complains that most therapists fail to focus on the pathological aspects of their patients' amusement; he recommends that any humor displayed by the patient be treated as symptomatic. He argues cogently that, when patients present with "smiling, laughter and a humorous attitude," (p. 423), they are frequently failing to take their condition seriously. He adds that such clinically relevant behaviors need to be understood as inappropriate defenses against emotions that are perhaps too frightening for the patient to deal with.

Obviously, laughter cannot cure disease. It can, however, provide symptom relief by reducing the natural stresses of illness and by providing a temporary distraction from anxiety. For those who find it a useful therapeutic tool, or for those who have been helped by it, there is no doubt that humor can provide a diversion from stress and pain. But is this kind of diversion really helpful? Is it really an oasis in the desert of illness, or just an illusory mirage that appears to bring relief, but in fact makes the suffering so much worse?

Anatole Broyard (1991) explains how "dying or illness is a kind of poetry. It's a derangement. In literary criticism they talk about the systematic derangement of the senses. This is what happens to the sick man" (p. 40). To engage oneself in the study of these dissociations and derangements seems so much more profitable and fascinating than distracting oneself by thinking about things that are "funny." Broyard, writing as a terminally ill cancer patient, claims he would like his ideal doctor to understand that beneath his surface cheerfulness, he feels what Ernest Becker called "the panic inherent in creation" and "the suction of infinity" (p. 42). Broyard implies that the terminally ill patient is closer to certain truths than any of us can be—is, in fact, hovering constantly on the brink of profound revelation—and the last thing he needs is to be distracted. The seriously ill person can understand, as no one else can, what Broyard describes as "the wonder, terror, and exaltation of being on the edge of being, between the natural and the supernatural" (p. 44).

Do such moments really benefit from the arrival of a clown wearing a red nose and brandishing a rubber chicken?

Afterword

"All right," said the Cat; and this time it vanished quite slowly, beginning with the end of the tail, and ending with the grin, which remained some time after the rest of it had gone.

"Well! I've often seen a cat without a grin," thought Alice; "but a grin without a cat! It's the most curious thing I ever saw in all my life!"

—Lewis Carroll, *Alice's Adventures in Wonderland*

Louis Wain was an English artist born in 1860 of mixed French and English parentage and most famous for his drawings of playful, anthropomorphic cats. By the turn of the century he had become a household name and was responsible for creating the "Louis Wain Cat," a special type of mischievous, cheeky feline. His irrepressibly cute cats and kittens were depicted dressed in human clothes, golfing, strolling, bathing, dancing, and sitting reluctantly at desks in the classroom. These corny illustrations were enormously popular and sold as cards, prints, and posters; the Louis Wain Annual was a perennial bestseller, and these cringingly sentimental creatures adorned countless postcards and filled the pages of newspapers, books, and periodicals. The Wain cat was ubiquitous, prompting H. G. Wells to remark that "English cats that do not look like Louis Wain cats are ashamed of themselves."

But things did not continue to go well for Wain. His wife, Emily, died prematurely from cancer, leaving the illustrator to provide for himself, his mother, and his five sisters. By 1890 he was working 14 hours a day to earn money to provide for his family; he was famous and much loved as an artist, but never very wealthy. Owing to his inattention to business matters, his cat pictures were often reproduced and sold without his permission. In 1900, one of Wain's five sisters, Marie, suffering from terrible delusions, was committed to a psychiatric institution. After the turn of the century, the demand for Louis Wain's cats began to diminish, but, unable to come to terms with the situation, Wain became increasingly obsessed with drawing them.

As time passed and his difficulties increased, Wain began to believe that spirits were directing malign energies against him. Isolated in the family home in Kilburn, London, ruminating on a series of fantastic electrical theories, he gradually became convinced that his sisters were conspiring to undermine his well-being. Finally, according to biographer Rodney Dale (1968), he grew psychotic, violent, and deranged, and in 1924, at the age of 64, was diagnosed as a schizophrenic and committed to the pauper ward of a South London asylum.

There, after a period of withdrawal, Wain began to paint again—as before, nothing but cats, hundreds and hundreds of cats. But something had happened to these cats. They were no longer happily capering around in top hats and tails but were brightly colored, unusually incandescent, and run through with a strange ecstatic electricity. In these later paintings, the cats' eyes became fixed with hostility, and their bodies collapsed into distorted and fantastic shapes (see Figure 4). Critic Geoff Cox (2001) gives a wonderful description of these later, "psychotic" cats:

Riotous and grinning or sublimely poised and inscrutable, their many-hued bright saucer eyes gaze from vistas of tangled foliage and pink-jeweled mountains. When shut indoors, they are set against intricate curlicues of wallpaper. On occasion, they fracture, shimmering into their ornate backgrounds. These are otherworld cats; always strange, joyous, unknowable and troubling [p. 18].

The last 15 years of Wain's life were spent in psychiatric asylums in the south of England: Springfield, Bethlem, and Napsbury. In these hos-

Normal Period

Psychotic Period

Stage One

Stage Two

Figure 4: Louis Wain Cats

pitals he continued to draw "psychotic" cats by the dozen, often as gifts for his warders. After a year of confinement he was accidentally "redis-covered" by bookseller and ward visitor Dan Rider, who drew public attention to Wain's impecunious condition, and a number of influential people and collectors of his work set up a fund to enable him to spend the rest of his days in relative comfort. Wain died in 1939 and is buried, alongside his family, in St. Mary's Roman Catholic Cemetery in Kensal Green, London.

Since Wain's "rediscovery" in the late 1960s, his work has been appro-priated by two main groups of people: cat lovers and those interested in "outsider art," particularly the art of schizophrenics. His work is espe-cially fascinating to those who study the art of the mentally ill because he had one main subject—cats—and numerous examples exist from both before and after Wain's illness. Today, in fact, Wain is better known as a schizophrenic than as a popular artist, mainly because his before-and-after cats have been reproduced in a number of psychology textbooks to illustrate the changes in the mental processing of psychotic personalities.

Wain's "psychotic" cats are generally regarded as a kind of oddity, appealing to our grotesque fascination with the darker side of life. As a result, their aesthetic value often goes unappreciated, as does the fact that these "psychotic" cats are actually a lot more interesting than their schmaltzy Victorian predecessors. There seems to be a kind of emotional truth about these pictures that is completely lacking from the earlier illus-trations, a reflection of the artist's psychotic breakdown.

Ironically, in an interview with Roy Compton (1896), Wain confessed that he was drawn to cats because he felt they were good for his mental health. He also described his belief that English housecats could be bred to have flatter, rounder faces. His description of the changes and attenu-ations to these cats' faces closely resembles the changes his own pictures of cats went through after his mental collapse:

> I have myself found . . . that all people who keep cats, and are in the habit of nursing them, do not suffer from those petty lit-tle ailments which all flesh is heir to, viz., nervous complaints of a minor sort. Hysteria and rheumatism, too, are unknown, and

all lovers of "pussy" are of the sweetest temperament. . . . Our English cats are slowly but surely developing into stronger types, which have very little affinity with the uncertain and unstable creature of the tiles and chimney-pots. With careful breeding the lank body and the long nose disappear, the face becomes condensed, as it were, into a series of circles, the expression develops artlessness, and the general temperament of the animal is one of loving conceit [p. 48].

It is Wain's "psychotic" cats that show the most genius in both inspiration and execution, and they are in many ways far more interesting than the earlier, cute Victorian felines. Most interesting about these "psychotic" cats, however, is their facial expression: more often than not a strange, demonic grin. This is not the pleasant smile of the calendar cats but an obsessive, hostile rictus, right on the edge of collapse into disarray. The once-soft forms of the cats have become formal and symmetrical, as if the artist were engaged in a desperate attempt to exert control over his mental functions.

In his most psychotic stage, the grins of Wain's cats widen so as to disintegrate completely, as if in a bizarre attempt to absorb all that appears before them. Their eyes expand and their form begins to dissolve. In the later pictures, nothing is left except a beautiful, symmetrical pattern, like a strange snowflake, in whose center are the remnants of a broad, wild grin.

Smiling, of course, is generally associated with sensations of pleasure. No one can deny that the human smile has an adaptive, evolutionary significance and a long history as a potent social signal that obviously promotes survival. For example, Newson and Newson (1963) have documented how parents who have seen their infant smile at them immediately feel gratification, and the amount of time they want to spend with their offspring automatically increases. There is also a contemporary literature on the relationship between neonatal and later social smiling, of which an early example is Emde, Gaensbauer, and Harmon's (1976) work on emotional expression in infancy. More recently, Keltner and Bonanno (1997) examined the ways in which smiling in adults facilitates the adaptive response to stress both by increasing the psychological distance from distress and by enhancing social relations.

If smiling is such a positive force, though, why does the fixed rictus, like that of Wain's "psychotic" cats, appear so frightening to us? The reason is clear: the fixed smile implies none of the pleasure normally associated with a "genuine" smile. In the fixed smile, the lights are on, but there's nobody home—at least, nobody we would want to meet. Like the evil clown, the fixed grin presents a façade of pleasure that conceals dark secrets.

Psychologists have convincingly argued that there can be facial expressions of emotion without the corresponding experience of that emotion (see Ekman, 1993) and that expressive facial displays are better predicted by social context than by emotional state (see Hess, Banse, and Kappas, 1995). As a result, a distinction has been made between what is sometimes referred to as the *Duchenne smile*, which involves the action of the orbicularis oculi muscles (the muscles around the eyes), and the *non-Duchenne smile*, which does not (see, e.g., Frank, Ekman, and Friesen, 1993). Studies have shown that Duchenne smiles correspond with self-reports of reduced anger and increased enjoyment, the dissociation of distress, better social relations, and positive responses from strangers; whereas non-Duchenne smiles are associated with none of these (Keltner and Bonnano, 1997). It also is important to add that, according to Ekman, Freisen, and O'Sullivan (1988), smiles that include traces of muscular actions associated with disgust, fear, contempt, or sadness occur most often when a person is trying to disguise negative emotions behind a "happy mask."

Victor Hugo's (1869) novel *The Man Who Laughs* contains a particularly fascinating example of the non-Duchenne smile. The infant Gwynplaine, remember, is a victim of a nomadic band of *comprachicos*— 17th-century child-buyers who specialized in turning children into freaks who could then be sold to sideshows or used lucratively as especially pitiful beggars:

> To succeed in producing a freak one must get hold of him early; a dwarf must be started when he is small. They stunted growth, they mangled features. It was an art/science of invented ortho-

pedics. Where nature had put a straight glance, this art put a squint. Where nature had put harmony, they put deformity and imperfection [p. 25].[1]

Historical evidence suggests that bands of *comprachicos* did actually exist in the 17th century, mainly in southern Europe, and carving the child's face into a permanent grin was actually one of their methods, although very rare. It was much more common, as Hugo suggests, for the *comprachicos* to create dwarves and similar monsters by growing living children in pots ("the child slowly fills the contours of the vase with compressed flesh and twisted bones" [p. 25]).[2] If these children could not be sold to a circus or private sideshow, they could earn a significant living (for their keepers) as beggars, since members of the public would gladly pay money to get such horrifying creatures out of their sight.

The non-Duchenne smile manufactured by the *comprachicos* is a terrifying literal manifestation of the popular belief that temporary facial expressions leave permanent traces, a fear also expressed in the folk admonition to children not to pull "funny faces" in case the wind changes and their faces remain that way. This fear is also at the heart of Ray Russell's (1961) haunting tale "Sardonicus." British critic John Carnell (1967) described it as "one of the greatest horror stories of recent times" (p. 31) and as clearly influenced by Victor Hugo's (1869) *The Man Who Laughs*.[3]

---

[1] Incidentally, Ayn Rand (1971) has a provocative essay on the *comprachicos*, in which she makes the case that "The New Left" are "the *comprachicos* of the mind" ("They do not place a child in a vase to adjust his body to its contours. They place him into a school to adjust him to society" [p. 88]).

[2] "This bottled development continues for several years," Hugo (1869) continues. "At a certain point, it becomes an irreparable monster. Then the vase is broken and one has a man in the shape of a pot" (p. 25). The practice apparently originated in ancient China and continues to the present day in certain parts of India, where "rat boys" created in this or similar fashion earn money for their keepers by begging and pickpocketing in grotesque hordes.

[3] On the big screen, "Sardonicus" became William Castle's *Mr. Sardonicus*, which was made in 1961. Tim Burton also claimed inspiration from Victor Hugo's *The Man Who Laughs* in his creation of the Joker, in his 1989 movie, *Batman*.

"Sardonicus" is the story of Marek Boleslawski, a young peasant who defies tradition and religion by digging up the corpse of his dead father to retrieve a winning lottery ticket accidentally buried along with the body. The ticket is retrieved, but at great cost; Boleslawski is forced to look directly upon the face of his dead father, whose cold lips are "drawn back from the teeth *in a constant and soul-shattering smile!*" (p. 50). Boleslawski is so traumatized by this encounter that his own face is permanently transformed into a replica of his dead father's, "the lips drawn back in a perpetual and mocking grin," the facial muscles immovable, "as if held in the gelid rigour of death" (p. 52). No longer able to pronounce his own name, Marek Boleslawski becomes the mysterious and evil Mr. Sardonicus, destined to spend his life hiding from the ridicule of others and desperately searching for a cure for his permanent *risus sardonicus*.

Finally, through nefarious means, Mr. Sardonicus obtains the private services of Sir Robert Cargrave, an expert in muscular paralysis, who injects his patient with a solution made by diluting a rare South American poison that kills by bringing about a total relaxation of the muscles, particularly the muscles of the lungs and heart. Sardonicus is cured—but not for long. He soon dies of starvation, incapable either of speaking, eating, or drinking because, it turns out, he is "absolutely unable to open his mouth" (p. 70). The key to the story comes when we learn that the solution Cargrave injected into Mr. Sardonicus's face was nothing but pure, distilled water. There was never anything corporeal wrong with Sardonicus's facial muscles; his punishment came "*not from God above or the Fiend below, but from within his own breast, his own brain, his own soul*" (p. 71).

A more contemporary but perhaps equally terrifying manifestation of the *risus sardonicus* could at one time be found at Coney Island's Dreamland, home of a ride known as the "Dragon's Cave," because above the entrance was a dragon's head that moved back and forth and breathed smoke through its mouth. Most memorable, however, was the entrance to the cave itself—a train track leading through an enormous, grinning clown's mouth with swinging doors. The rest of the clown's face was highly garish, with lots of flashing red lights on a big red nose. "The Dragon's Cave," apparently one of the most hair-raising and best constructed rides at Dreamland, took passengers through quite a few sets of doors into five or six different rooms. Plenty of kids experienced their first *frisson* of true horror as their carriage smashed open the dark swinging doors and carried them into the nightmare of that clown's terrible grin.

And, then, in the small hours of the morning on May 27, 1911, a fire broke out in "Hell's Gate," a boat ride into a bottomless pit. According to historian Judith Adams (1991), Coney Island had no proper fire extinguishing system, and strong winds caused the inferno to tear through Dreamland's lathe-and-plaster buildings, the "uncontrolled flames leaping higher than any of Coney's towers, animals screaming from within cages where they were trapped to burn to death, and crazed lions . . . running with burning manes through the streets" (p. 41). After the conflagration was over, one of the few structures that remained of the original funfair was the huge clown's grin at the Dragon's Lair, which remained uncannily intact after the entire funfair around it had burned completely to the ground.

These images of the disembodied rictus clearly represent the important connections outlined by Legman between laughter and horror. To understand their implications fully, we must now turn to the work of the Russian critic Mikhail Bakhtin (1968, 1971, 1981) and his progressive reading of that state of mind and body known as "carnival." It may seem rather perverse and contradictory to analyze such a frightening facial expression as the non-Duchenne smile in the light of a theory as apparently positive as Bakhtinian carnivalesque. I would argue, however, that the Bakhtinian carnivalesque readily embraces pain, suffering, negativity, and horror without necessarily transforming them into positive, life-affirming experiences. All too often, Bakhtin's reading of the carnival is misunderstood and "secularized"—not unlike Freudian psychoanalysis—into an optimistic celebration of social and linguistic diversity, a mere festival of difference; many critics have drawn attention to Bakhtin's romantic populism. However, while it is certainly true that Bakhtin tended to downplay the more macho-aggressive aspects of the carnival and overstate its antipatrician optimism, he was highly conscious of the darker elements of the carnival and moreover was entirely prepared for his theories to be applied to other genres, fields, and modes in times and places yet unknown to him.[4]

---

[4] "The unity of the emerging (developing) idea," noted Bakhtin in 1971. "Hence a certain *internal* open-endedness. . . . Sometimes it is difficult to separate one open-endedness from another" (p. 155).

Etymologists have argued at length about the origins of the word *carnival*. Some claim a derivation from the phrase *carne levare*, "the solace of the flesh"; others claim a relation with *carne vale*, "a farewell to flesh"; yet others claim origins in the expression *carne avale*, "down with flesh!" It is agreed virtually beyond doubt, however, that the word originally derives from the phrase *carnem levare*, "the putting away or removal of flesh" (as food) in the season immediately preceding Lent, on the eve of Ash Wednesday. The removal of flesh—what better way to describe the rictus grin that endures when all else is gone, reminding us of nothing more than what the poet T. S. Eliot (1963), writing about the Elizabethan dramatist John Webster, referred to as "the skull beneath the skin"?

The static rictus grin is a carnivalesque image because it suggests a world turned inside out. According to Bakhtin (1968, 1971, 1981), carnival is a time of ritual reversal, an institutional time of upheaval when ordinary people become horrifying monsters or animals and the dead are resurrected. The element of relativity and *becoming* is emphasized, in opposition to the immovable and extratemporal stability of the medieval hierarchy. A principal function of the medieval carnival was to emphasize the importance of inside-out and upside-down in the movements and acts of the body. Bakhtin (1968) refers to carnival as a parody of truth in a world which is "turned inside out" (p. 95).

Bakhtin also points out that one of the most significant features of the carnival is the way in which, at carnival time, death becomes comic, as in the Rabelaisian mocking of death. The Rabelaisian carnival presents a number of examples of the grotesque or *clownish* portrayal of death, and the image of death takes on humorous aspects. Bakhtin (1981) points out that "death is inseparable from *laughter*" (p. 196). And so we arrive at the presentation of *cheerful deaths*. The rictus grin of Louis Wain's "psychotic" cats, for example, is a highly carnivalesque representation, as Bakhtin (1968) suggests:

> Of all the features of the human face, the nose and mouth play the most important part in the grotesque image of the body; the head, ears and nose also acquire a grotesque character when they adopt the animal form or that of inanimate objects. . . . But the

more important of all human features for the grotesque is the mouth. It dominates all else. The grotesque face is actually reduced to the gaping mouth; the other features are only a frame encasing this wide-open bodily abyss [p. 316].

As the work of Gershon Legman has helped us to understand, smiles, humor, and laughter can all provide us with temporary distractions, deluding us that the human condition is not such a serious one. Most people do not like to be surrounded by solemnity, especially when introversion would force them to come to face themselves and their own neuroses and anxieties. How better to disguise one's crippling facial disfigurement than with the whimsical delight of a clown's red nose?

One of the notable hallmarks of contemporary Western culture is that denial of the human condition is regarded as necessary to sustain mental health, rather than being a symptom of psychopathology. The acceptance of denial under the guise of "humor" not only makes regression possible, but hides the underlying censored impulse. It is probably for this reason that any kind of analysis of "humor" usually meets with such strong resistance. We like to "enjoy ourselves" without thinking about what we are doing or what this "enjoyment" involves. We are afraid that, if we examine our "enjoyment" too closely, what we discover will spoil it, and put an end to our "fun." The success of humor, like that of a dream, depends on the effectiveness of the disguise of its real instinctual aims—which is why many people find it difficult to remember jokes, just as they find it difficult to remember their dreams upon waking. Psychotic persons, who in some respects see more clearly than the rest of us, are not great joke-tellers, and will often react to "humor" with revulsion because they see too clearly its tragic aggression and undisguised pain.

Like stand-up comedians, those who feel compelled to tell jokes and act "humorously" in social situations are often expressing almost openly the despair and hostility of their need for attention by forcing their various forms of "entertainment" on audiences who are generally willing to grant them that attention. Usually, these people are known to be "funny," which is often their only social "grace" and the only way they know of dealing with other human beings.

For some, humor causes deep unease; for others, it causes great pleasure. The German analyst Otto Fenichel (1945) maintained that a response by laughter is far better evidence of the correctness of an interpretation than is either a "yes" or a "no." Humor and laughter render acceptable ideas that could not otherwise be discussed without enormous discomfort; and, when humor is "successful," as Legman explains, the repressed can become conscious without excessive anxiety.

Distraction and denial are important components of what we describe as "entertainment," the term that is most commonly applied to grim and depressing fantasies. Most popular "entertainment" seems to involve some kind of mastery by denial. Indeed, the very themes most provocative of anxiety are precisely the most common themes of popular "entertainment"—sex, violence, the body, human relationships—as though to laugh at something is to deny that it arouses anxiety; just as, according to Legman, the motive for telling a joke always consists of an attempt to get the approval of the audience for the underlying guilt about the offensive impulses concealed in the joke. Most modern forms of "entertainment," in fact, consist of the public description or enactment of acts and deeds that for many people—perhaps most of all the "entertainers" themselves—are the wellsprings of deep private shame and humiliation.

There is nothing we human beings enjoy more than a "good laugh." People are always looking to something funny to "take their minds off it," at least for a while. "It" may be something trivial or something important, depending on immediate circumstances, but in the end, of course, "it" is always and only death. Only through death can we know that the human smile is the shadow of the skull's hollow grin.

References

Adams, J. A. (1991), *The American Amusement Park Industry: A History of Technology and Thrills*. Boston: Twayne.

Addison, J. (1712), Editorial. *The Spectator,* September 26:2–4.

Allport, G. W. (1937), *Personality: A Psychological Interpretation*. London: Constable.

Anonymous (1969), Review of *The Humor of Hostility*. *Time,* January 17:43.

——— (1971), Review of *Rationale of the Dirty Joke. Psychoanal. Rev.*, 58:644.

Arieti, S. (1950), New views on the psychology and psychopathology of wit and of the comic. *Psychiatry*, 13:43–48.

Arlazaroff, A., Mester, R., Spivak, B., Klein, C. & Toren, P. (1998), Pathological laughter: Common vs. unusual aetiology and presentation. *Israel J. Psychiatry & Related Sci.*, 35:84–189.

Austin, R. K. ("Happy") & McCann, U. D. (1996), Ballatrophobia: When clowns aren't funny [letter]. *Anxiety*, 2:305.

Bakhtin, M. M. (1968), *Rabelais and His World* (trans. H. Iswolsky). Cambridge, MA: MIT Press.

——— (1971), *Speech Genres and Other Late Essays*, ed. C. Emerson & M. Holquist (trans. V. W. McGee). Austin: University of Texas Press, 1986.

——— (1981), *The Dialogic Imagination* (trans. C. Emerson & M. Holquist). Austin: University of Texas Press.

Bancroft, J., Johnson, C. & Stirratt, B., eds. (2001), *Sex and Humor: Collections from the Kinsey Institute*. Bloomington: Indiana University Press.

Baudelaire, C. (1855), *The Essence of Laughter and Other Essays, Journals and Letters*, ed. P. Quemell. Chicago: Northwestern University Press, 1936.

Bergson, H. (1911), *Laughter: An Essay on the Meaning of the Comic* (trans. C. Breretson). New York: Macmillan, 1926.

Braddock, L. E. & Heard, R. N. S. (1986), Visual hallucinations due to indomethacin: A case report. *Internat. Clin. Psychopharmacol.*, 1:26–270.

Brody, M. W. (1950), The meaning of laughter. *Psychoanal. Quart.*, 19:192–201.

Brophy, B. (1969), Superman's trousers: Review of *Rationale of the Dirty Joke* by G. Legman. *The Listener*, September 11:350–351.

Brottman, M. (2001a), Gershon Legman: Lord of the lewd. In: *Sex and Humor: Collections from the Kinsey Institute*, ed. J. Bancroft, C. Johnson & B. Stirratt. Bloomington: Indiana University Press, pp. 42–53.

———(2001b), The evil clown: Autopsy of an archetype. Presented at Columbia University Seminar for Cinema and Interdisciplinary Interpretation, December 6.

———(2002), Risus sardonicus: Neurotic and pathological laughter. *Humor*, 15:401–417.

Broyard, A. (1991), *Intoxicated by My Illness*. New York: Clarkson Potter.

Buehler, R. E. (1970), Review of *Rationale of the Dirty Joke* by G. Legman. *J. Amer. Folklore*, 83:87.

Bukatman, S. (1993), *Terminal Identity: The Virtual Subject in Postmodern Science Fiction*. Durham, NC: Duke University Press.

Byron, C. (1976), Killing laughter. *Time*, August 2.

Cahill, T. with Ewing, R. (1986), *Buried Dreams: Inside the Mind of a Serial Killer*. New York: Bantam Books.

Calhoun, J. B.(1972), Plight of the Ik and Kaiadilt is seen as a chilling possible end for man. *Smithsonian*, 3(8):19–23.

Carnell, J. (1967), Introduction. In: *Sardonicus: The Playboy Book of Horror and the Supernatural* by R. Russell. Chicago: Playboy Enterprises, p. 31.

Carpy, D.V. (1989), Tolerating the countertransference: A mutative process. *Internat. J. Psycho-Anal.*, 70:278–294.

Carroll, L. (1865), *Alice's Adventures in Wonderland, and Through the Looking Glass*. London: Penguin, 1998.

Carter, A. (1984), *Nights at the Circus*. London: Vintage.

Chervet, B .(1996), Cycle de la latence, clivage du moi et conversion mystique. *Rev. Française de la Psychanalyse*, 60:1585–1596.

Chesterfield, Lord (1774), *Lord Chesterfield's Letters*. Oxford: Oxford University Press, 1988.

Cicero (55 B.C.), *De Oratore*, ed. & trans. E. W. Sutton & H. Rackham, 2 vols. Cambridge, MA: Harvard University Press, 1969.

Cirlot, J. E. (1971), *A Dictionary of Symbols*. New York: Dorset Press.

Cohen, T. (1999), *Jokes: Philosophical Thoughts on Joking Matters*. Chicago: University of Chicago Press.

Coleman, J. (1972), Cop-you-lay-shun. *The New Statesman*, February 11:180–181.

Comics Magazine Association of America Comics Code (1954), Code for Editorial Matter, General Standards Part A, paragraph 7.

Compton, R. (1896), A chat with Louis Wain. *The Idler*, 8:48–52.

Coppens, A. (pseud. Nicholas Schors) (1969), *Memoirs of an Erotic Bookseller*. London: Skilton.

Cornog, M. & Perper, T. (1999), Make love not war: The legacy of Gershon Legman, 1917-1999. *J. Sex Res.*, 36:316–317.

Cornwell, D. & Hobbs, S. (1988), Hunting the monster with iron teeth. In: *Monsters with Iron Teeth*, ed. G. Bennett & P. Smith. Sheffield, UK: Sheffield Academic Press, pp. 115–137.

Cousins, N. (1979), *Anatomy of an Illness as Perceived by the Patient*. New York: Norton.

Cowley, M. (1949), Sex, censorship and Superman: Review of *Love & Death*. *New Republic*, October 10:18–19.

Cox, G. (2001), Bizarre lives: Louis Wain. *Bizarre*, October 18.

Dale, R. (1968), *Louis Wain—The Man Who Drew Cats*. London: William Kimber.

Daniels, E. B., Jr. (1973), Notes on clowns, madness and psychotherapy. *J. Psychother. & Psychosomat.*, 24:465–470.

Davis, S. (2002), Gershon Legman confronts the post office. *Counterpunch*, October/November 4–9.

Dery, M. (1999), *The Pyrotechnic Insanitarium*. New York: Grove Press.

Descartes, R. (1649), *The Passions of the Soul* (trans. S. H. Voss). Paris: Hackett, 1989.

Douglas, M. (1978), *Implicit Meanings: Essays in Anthropology*. London: Routledge & Kegan Paul.

Driscoll, R. (1987), Humor in pragmatic psychotherapy. In: *Handbook of Humor and Psychotherapy*, ed. W. F. Fry Jr. & W. A. Salameh. Sarasota, FL: Professional Resource Exchange, pp. 127–149.

Dudar, H.(1984), Love, death and schmutz: Gershon Legman's second thoughts. *Village Voice*, May 1:41–43.

Dundes, A. (1965), Review of *The Horn Book: Studies in Erotic Folklore and Bibliography* by G. Legman. *J. Amer. Folklore*, 78:161.

Dunsany, Lord (1916), *The Last Book of Wonder*. Boston: John W. Luce.

Eastman, M. (1936), *Enjoyment of Laughter*. New York: Simon & Schuster.

Ekman, P. (1993), Facial expression and emotion. *Amer. Psychol.*, 48:384–392.

——— Freisen, W. V. & O'Sullivan, M. (1988), Smiles when lying. *J. Personal. & Soc. Psychol.*, 54:414–420.

Eliade, M. (1974), *Man and the Sacred*. New York: Harper & Row.

Eliot, T. S. (1963), Whispers of immortality. In: *Collected Poems 1909–1962*. New York: Harcourt Brace.

Ellis, A. (1984), How to deal with your most difficult client—you. *Psychother. in Private Prac.*, 2:25–35.

———(1987), The use of rational humorous songs in psychotherapy. In: *Handbook of Humor and Psychotherapy*, ed. W. F. Fry Jr. & W. A.Salameh. Sarasota, FL: Professional Resource Exchange, pp. 265–285.

Emde, R. N., Gaensbauer, T. S. & Harmon, R. J. (1976), *Emotional Expression in Infancy: A Biobehavioral Study*. Psychological Issues Monogr. 37. New York: International Universities Press.

Farrelly, F. & Lynch, M. (1987), Humor in provocative therapy. In: *Handbook of Humor and Psychotherapy*, ed. W. F. Fry Jr. & W. A. Salameh. Sarasota, FL: Professional Resource Exchange, pp. 81–107.

Feiner, A. H. (1995), Laughter among the pear trees: Vengeance, vindictiveness and vindication. *Contemp. Psychoanal.*, 31:381–397.

Fenichel, O. (1945), *The Psychoanalytic Theory of Neurosis*. New York: Norton.

Frank, M. G., Ekman, P. & Friesen, W. (1993), Behavioral markers and recognizability of the smile of enjoyment. *J. Personal. & Soc. Psychol.*, 64:83–93.

Frankl, V. E. (1946), *Man's Search for Meaning*, New York: Washington Square Press, 1997.

———(1967), *The Doctor and the Soul*. New York: Bantam.

Franklin, B. & Legman, G. (1949), *David Ricardo and Ricardian Theory: A Bibliographical Checklist*. New York: Burt Franklin.

Franzini, L. R. (2001), Humor in therapy: The case for training therapists in its uses and risks. *J. Gen. Psychol.*, 128:170–197.

French, P. (1969), Digging the dirt: Review of *Rationale of the Dirty Joke. New Statesman*, August 29:278–279.

Freud, S. (1900), The interpretation of dreams. *Standard Edition*, 4 & 5. London: Hogarth Press, 1953.

———(1905), Jokes and their relation to the unconscious. *Standard Edition*, 8:9–236. London: Hogarth Press, 1960.

———(1909), Analysis of a phobia in a five-year-old boy. *Standard Edition*, 10:5–149. London: Hogarth Press, 1955.

———(1913), Totem and taboo. *Standard Edition*, 13:1–161. London: Hogarth Press, 1955.

———(1927), Humor. *Standard Edition*, 21:161–166. London: Hogarth Press, 1961.

——— (1930), Civilization and its discontents. *Standard Edition*, 21:64–145. London: Hogarth Press, 1961.

Fry, W. F., Jr. & Salameh, W. A., eds. (1987), *Handbook of Humor and Psychotherapy*. Sarasota, FL: Professional Resource Exchange.

Gacy, J. W. with McClelland, C. I. (1995), *Question of Doubt*. New York: Craig Bowles.

Goldstein, J. H. (1987), Therapeutic effects of laughter. In: *Handbook of Humor and Psychotherapy*, ed. W. F. Fry Jr. & W. A. Salameh. Sarasota, FL: Professional Resource Exchange, pp. 15–28.

Gregory, J. (1924), *The Nature of Laughter*. London: Kegan Paul.

Grieg, J. (1923), *The Psychology of Laughter and Comedy*. London: Allen & Unwin.

Griffiths, T. (1976), *Comedians*. New York: Grove Press.

Grotjahn, M. (1949), Laughter in psychoanalysis. *Samiska*, 3:76–82.

———(1957), *Beyond Laughter*. New York: Blakiston.

——— (1972), Sexuality and humor—Don't laugh! *Psychol. Today*, July:51–53.

Hamilton, G. V. & Legman, G. (1950), *On the Cause of Homosexuality: Two Essays, the Second in Reply to the First*. New York: Breaking Point.

Hess, U., Banse, R. & Kappas, P. (1995), The intensity of facial expression is determined by underlying affective state and social situation. *J. Personal. & Soc. Psychol.*, 69:280–288.

Hobbes. T. (1652), *Leviathan*. New York: Viking, 1982.

Hoffmann, F. (1967), Review of *The Horn Book. Studies in Erotic Folklore and Bibliography* by G. Legman. *Western Folklore*, 26:61–62.

Holmes, J.C. (1967), *Nothing More to Declare*. New York: Dutton.

Huizinga, J. (1944), *Homo Ludens: A Study of the Play Element in Culture*. Boston, MA: Beacon Press, 1955.

Hugo, V. (1869), *The Man Who Laughs*. Boston: Dana Estes.

Jackson, B. (1977), Legman: King of X700. *Maledicta*, 1:112.

———(1980), Erotic lore: Review of *The New Limerick. J. Amer. Folklore*, 9:209.

Jacobson, H. (1996), *Seriously Funny: From the Ridiculous to the Sublime*. London: Viking Press.

Janus, S. S. (1975), The great comedians: Personality and other factors. *Amer. J. Psychoanal.*, 35:169–174.

Jarry, A. (1898), *Ubu Roi [King Turd]* (trans. G. Legman & B. Keith). New York: Dover, 1953.

Jenkins, R. S. (1994), *Subversive Laughter: The Liberating Power of Comedy*. New York: Free Press.

Jolley, G. M. (1982), The use of humor in psychotherapy. Unpub. Master's thesis, California State University, Hayward.

Jones, J. H. (1997), *Alfred C. Kinsey: A Public / Private Life*. London: Norton.

Kaplan, H. B. & Boyd, I. H.(1965), The social functions of humor on an open psychiatric ward. *Psychiat. Quart.*, 39:502–515.

Philip Kaplan Collection, Accession II, Special Collections, Southern Illinois University Library, Carbondale.

Kass, R. (1953), Jerry Lewis analyzed. *Films in Review*, 4:119–123.

Kazdin, A. E. (1999), Humor in therapy [letter to the editor]. *Amer. Psycholog. Assn. Monitor*, 5:3.

Kearney, P. (1981), *The Private Case: An Annotated Bibliography of the Private Case Erotica Collection in the British (Museum) Library*. St. Louis, MO: J. Landesman.

Keltner, D. & Bonnano, G. A. (1997), A study of laughter and dissociation: Distinct correlates of laughter and smiling during bereavement. *J. Personal. & Soc. Psychol.*, 73:687–702.

Alfred Kinsey Collection, Kinsey Institute Library, Indiana University, Bloomington.

Kinsey, A. C. et al. (1948), *Sexual Behavior in the Human Male*. Bloomington: Indiana University Press.

——— (1953), *Sexual Behavior in the Human Female*. Bloomington: Indiana University Press.

Kivy, P. (2003), Jokes are a laughing matter. *J. Aesthetics & Art Crit.*, 61:5–17.

Klapp, O. E. (1950), The fool as a social type. *Amer. J. Sociol.*, 55:157–162.

Klauber, J. (1986), Elements of the psychoanalytic relationship and their therapeutic implications. In: *British School of Psychoanalysis*, ed. G. Kohon. London: Free Association Press, pp. 200–213.

Klein, A. (1989), *The Healing Power of Humor*. New York: Putnam.

——— (1998), *The Courage to Laugh*. New York: Putnam.

Knobel, P. (1999), Gershon Legman [obituary]. *The Australian*, March 31, p.15.

Kris, E. (1940), Laughter as an expressive process. *Internat. J.Psycho-Anal.*, 21:314–141.

——— (1952), *Psychoanalytic Explorations in Art*. New York: International Universities Press.

Kristeva, J. (1982), *Powers of Horror: An Essay on Abjection* (trans. L. S. Roudiez). New York: Columbia University Press.

Kubie, L. (1971), The destructive potential of humor in psychotherapy. *Amer. J. Psychiatry*, 127:861–866.

LaFrance, M. (1983), Felt versus feigned funniness: Issues in coding smiling and laughing. In: *Handbook of Humor Research, Vol. 1*, ed. P. E. McGhee & J. H. Goldstein. New York: Springer, pp. 1–12.

Jay Landesman Papers, Special Collections, Library of the University of Missouri, St. Louis.

Landesman, J. (1987), *Rebel Without Applause*. New York: Permanent Press.

———— & Legman, G., eds. (1948), *Neurotica*. St. Louis, MO: J. Landesman. Repr. 1963 as *The Compleat Neurotica*. New York: Hacker Art Books.

Legman, G. (1940) [pseud. R.-M. de la Glannège], *Oragenitalism: An Encyclopaedic Outline of Oral Techniques in Genital Excitation, Part 1: Cunnilingus*. New York: J. R. Brussel; 2nd ed., rev. & enlgd. 1969, New York: Julian Press. Repr. 1971 as *The Intimate Kiss*, New York: Paperback Library; 1972, London: Duckworth: Trans: French 1970 Paris: Truong; German 1970 Flensburg Stephenson; Dutch 1971 Uithoorn: Nieuwe Wieken; Japanese 1972 Fujisawa: Ikeda Shoten.

———— (1948a) [pseud. N. Lockridge], *The Sexual Conduct of Men and Women: A Minority Report*. London: Hogarth Press. Repr. pbk. 1956 as *Sex Without Tears*. London: Bridgehead Books.

———— (1948b), The psychopathology of the comics. *Neurotica*, 3:3–30. Repr. 1949 as "Not For Children" in *Love & Death*. Trans. 1948 French: La psychopathologies des bandes dessineés. *Les Temps Modernes*, May 31.

———— (1949), *Love & Death: A Study in Censorship*. New York: Breaking Point. Repr. 1985 New York: Hacker Books.

———— (1950a), Le bitch-heroine. *Les Temps Modernes*, August 58.

———— (1950b), By popular demand. *Neurotica*, 6:45–47.

———— (1951), Rationale of the dirty joke. *Neurotica*, 9:49–64.

———— (1952a), *Bibliography of Paper-Folding*. Malvern, UK: Priory Press.

———— (1952b), Lotus and bow-tie. *Phoenix*. March 21:1003–1004.

———— (1952c), Paper-folding. *Magicol*, May 11:34–36.

———— (1952d), Lingam and yoni. *Phoenix*. April 24:785–785.

———— (1953), *The Limerick: 1700 Examples, with Notes, Variants and Index* [anon.]. Paris: Les Hautes Etudes. Repr. pbk. 1970 New York: Brandywine Press; 1974 London: Jupiter Books/New York: Bell; 1976 New York: Panther Books; 1978 New York: Castle Books.

———(1961a). Preface. In: *Ma Vie Secrète*. Paris: Cercle du Livre Précieux. Repr. 1969 Paris: L'Or du Temps.

———(1961b), Review of Alan Lomax's *Folksongs of North America in the English Language*. *J. Amer. Folklore*, 74:265–268.

———(1962a), *Unexpurgated Folk-Balladry, British and American: Bibliographical Check-List, Part II. 1800–1961*. Author: Valbonna, FR.

———(1962b), Preface. In: *Bibliography of Prohibited Books* by Pisanus Fraxi [pseud. of H. S. Ashbee]. New York: Jack Brussel.

———(1962c), Introduction. In: *Les Chansons de Salle de Garde*. Paris: Cercle du Livre Précieux.

———(1962d), Who owns folklore? *Western Folklore*, 21:1–12.

———(1962e), Toward a motif-index of erotic humor. *J. Amer. Folklore*, 75:227–248.

——— (1964a), *The Horn Book: Studies in Erotic Folklore and Bibliography*. New Hyde Park, NY: repr. 1966 New Hyde Park, NY: University Books; 1970 London: Jonathan Cape. Trans: Spanish 1974 Mexico City: Ediciones Roca.

——— (1964b), Introduction. In: *Merry Songs and Ballads*, ed. J. F. Farmer. New York: Cooper Square.

———(1966a), Introduction. In: *Dictionary of Slang and Its Analogues*, rev., comp. & ed. J. S. Farmer & W. E. Henley. New Hyde Park, NY: University Books, pp. xxx–xciv.

———(1966b), Introduction. In: *Russian Secret Tales: Bawdy Folktales of Old Russia*, ed. A. Afransyev. New York: Brussel & Brussel.

———(1966c), Introduction. *My Secret Life* by anon. New York: Grove Press.

———(1966d), *The Guilt of the Templars*. New York: Basic Books. Trans: French 1970 Paris: Tchou, Repr. 1973 Paris: Veyrier.

———(1967), *The Fake Revolt*. New York: Breaking Point.

——— (1968), *Rationale of the Dirty Joke: An Analysis of Sexual Humor, 1st series*. New York: Grove Press. Repr. pbk. 1969 London: Jonathan Cape, 1971 New York: Grove Press; 1972 2 vols. pbk. London: Panther Books. Trans. French 1971 Paris: R. Laffont; Italian 1972–1973, Rimini: Guaraldi.

———(1975), *No Laughing Matter: Rationale of the Dirty Joke, 2nd series*. New York: Breaking Point. Repr. 1978 London: Hart-Davis McGibbon; 1982 Bloomington: Indiana University Press.

————(1977a), *The New Limerick: 2750 Unpublished Examples, American and British*. New York: Crown.

————(1977b), A word for it! *Maledicta,* 1:9–18.

————(1977c), *Italian and Venetian Profanity* by G. Averna (coll. & trans. G. Legman). *Maledicta,* 1:63–64.

———— (1981), Introduction. In: *The Private Case: An Annotated Bibliography of the Private Case Erotica Collection in the British (Museum) Library*. St. Louis, MO: J. Landesman.

———— (1991), Erotica bibliography. In: *Libraries, Erotica and Pornography*, ed. M. Cornog. Phoenix, AZ: Oryx.

————(1992), Introduction. In: *Roll Me in Your Arms and Blow the Candle Out—"Unprintable" Ozark Folksongs and Folklore*, ed. V. Rudolph & G. Legman. Fayetteville: University of Arkansas Press.

———— & Sewall, R. (1971a), *An Oxford Thesis on Love* by L. Erectus Mentulus. New York: Grove Press.

———— & ———— (1971b), *The Oxford Professor Returns and Torrid Tales* by L. Erectus Mentulus. New York: Venus Library.

Levine, J. (1961), Regression in primitive clowning. *Psychoanal. Quart.,* 30:72–83.

Lewis, R. (2002), *The Other Great Depression*. New York: Plume.

Limon, J. (2000), *Stand-up Comedy in Theory, or Abjection in America*. Durham, NC: Duke University Press.

Louapre, D. & Sweetman, D. (1989), *Beautiful Stories for Ugly Children 1: A Cotton Candy Autopsy*. New York: Piranha Press.

Lott, E. (1993), *Love and Theft: Blackface Minstrelsy and the American Working Class*. Oxford: Oxford University Press.

Ludovici, A. M. (1933), *The Secret of Laughter*. New York: Viking Press.

Mahony, D. (2000), Is laughter the best medicine, or any medicine at all? *Eye on Psi Chi,* 2:18–31.

Mann, T. (1912), *Death in Venice and Other Stories* (trans. D. Luke). New York: Bantam, 1988.

————(1954), *The Confessions of Felix Krull, Confidence Man* (trans. D. Lindley). New York: Knopf, 1992.

Marcos, L. (1974), The emotional correlates of smiling and laughter: A preliminary research study. *Amer. J. Psychoanal.,* 34:33–42.

Marcus, N. N. (1990), Treating those who fail to take themselves seriously: Pathological aspects of humor. *Amer. J. Psychother.*, 44:423–432.

Maturin, C. R. (1821), *Melmoth the Wanderer.* Oxford : Oxford University Press, 1989.

McGhee, P. E. (1983), The role of arousal and hemispheric lateralization in humor. In: *Handbook of Humor Research, Vol. 1*, ed. P. E. McGhee & J. H. Goldstein. New York: Springer, pp. 21–28.

———— & Goldstein, J. H., eds. (1983), *Handbook of Humor Research, Vol.1.* New York: Springer.

Mendez, M. F., Nakawatase, T. V. & Brown, C. V. (1999), Involuntary laughter and inappropriate hilarity. *J. Neuropsychiatry & Clin. Neurosci.*, 11:253–258.

Moran, G. S. (1987), Some functions of play and playfulness—A developmental perspective. *The Psychoanalytic Study of the Child*, 42:11–29. New Haven, CT: Yale University Press.

Morreall, J. (1982), *Taking Laughter Seriously.* Albany: State University of New York Press.

Nasso, C. (1977), G(ershon) Legman. *Contemporary Authors, Vol. 21*, rev. Detroit, MI: Gale Research, p. 526.

Newson, J. & Newson, E. (1963), *Infant Care in an Urban Community.* London: Allen & Unwin.

Nietzsche, F. W. (1901), *The Will to Power.* New York: Random House, 1987.

O'Connell, W. E. (1987), Natural high theory and practice: The humorist's game of games. In: *Handbook of Humor and Psychotherapy*, ed. W. F. Fry Jr. & W. A. Salameh. Sarasota, FL: Professional Resource Exchange, pp. 55–81.

Peter, L. J. & Dana, B. (1998), *The Laughter Prescription: The Tools of Humor and How to Use Them.* New York: Ballantine Books.

Pfeifer, K. (1994), Laughter and pleasure. *Humor*, 7:57–172.

Piaget, J. (1951), *Play, Dreams and Imitation in Childhood.* London: Heinemann.

Plato (370–375 B.C.), *The Republic* (trans B. Jowett). New York: Collier & Son.

Poe, E. A. (1845), *Selected Tales*. Oxford: Oxford University Press, 1998.

Poland, W. S. (1990), The gift of laughter: The development of a sense of humor in clinical analysis. *Psychoanal. Quart.*, 59:197–225.

Pomeroy, W. B. (1972), *Dr. Kinsey and the Institute for Sex Research*. New York: Harper & Row.

Poznar, W. (1983) The apocalyptic vision in Nathanael West's *Miss Lonelyhearts*. In: *Apocalyptic Visions Past and Present*, ed. J. James & W. J. Cloonan. Tallahassee: Florida State University Press.

Prévost, M. (2002), *Rictus Romantiques: Politiques du Rire Chez Victor Hugo*, Montreal, CAN: Montreal University Press.

Rand, A. (1971), *The New Left—The Anti-Industrial Revolution*. New York: New American Library.

Redlich, F. C., Levine, J. & Sohler, T. P. (1951), A mirth response test: Preliminary report on a psychodiagnostic technique utilizing dynamics of humor. *Amer. J. Orthopsychiat.*, 21:717–734.

Reich, W. (1946), *Mass Psychology of Fascism*. New York: Orgone Institute Press.

———— (1968), *Function of the Orgasm*. London: Panther.

Reynolds, R. (1992), *Only the Truth Is Funny*. New York: Hyperion.

Richman, J. (1996), Jokes as a projective technique: The humor of psychiatric patients. *Amer. J. Psychother.*, 50:336–347.

————& Mango, C. R. (1990), Humor and art therapy. *Amer. J. Art Ther.*, 28:111–116.

Riesman, J. (1998), *Kinsey: Crimes and Consequences*. Crestwood, KY: Institute for Media Education.

Rose, C. (2002), Catching the ball: The role of play in psychoanalytic treatment. *J. Amer. Psychoanal. Assn.*, 50:1299–1309.

Russell, R. (1961), Sardonicus. In: *The Playboy Book of Horror and the Supernatural*. Chicago: Playboy Enterprises, 1967, pp. 31–54.

Russell, R. E. (1996), Understanding laughter in terms of basic perceptual and response patterns. *Humor*, 9:48–56.

Rycroft, C. (1969), What's so funny? Review of *Rationale of the Dirty Joke*. *New York Rev. Books*, April 10, pp. 24–25.

Sacks, O. (1997), Commentary on pathological laughter to the authors. *Israel J. Psychiatry & Related Sci.*, 35:189.

Salameh, W. A. (1993), Teaching clinical humor. *Humor & Health Letter*, 2(May/June):1–5.

———— (1994), Humor immersion training. *Humor & Health Letter*, 3(January/February):1–5.

Sanders, B. (1995), *Sudden Glory—Laughter as Subversive History*. Boston, Beacon Press.

Sanville, J. (1991), *The Playground of Psychoanalytic Therapy*. Hillsdale, NJ: The Analytic Press.

Saper, B. (1987), Humor in psychotherapy: Is it good or bad for the client? *Profess. Psychol.: Res. & Prac.*, 18:360–367.

Sarris, A. (1968), *The American Cinema: Directors and Directions 1929–1968*. New York: Dutton.

Schiller, F. (1795), *Letters upon the Aesthetic Education of Man*. New Haven, CT: Yale University Press, 1954.

Schopenauer, A. (1859), *The World as Will and Representation*, 2 vols. (trans. E. F. Payne). London: Dover, 1969.

Scott, J. (1999), Gershon Legman [obituary]. *New York Times*, March 14, p. 24.

Searles, H. F. (1979), *Countertransference and Related Subjects*. Madison, CT: International Universities Press.

Seligmann, S. (1910), *Der Böser Blick und Verwandtes. Ein Beitrag zur Geschichte des Aberglaubens alter Zeiten und Völker*. Berlin: Herman-Bardsdorf.

Sewall, R. (1981), *The Sign of the Scorpion: An Erotic Mystery Story*. New York: Grove Press.

Shafquat, S., Elkind, M. S. V., Chiocca, E. A., Takeoka, M. & Koroshetz, W. J. (1998), Petroclival meningioma presenting with pathological laughter. *Neurology*, 50:1918–1919.

Shaibani, A. T., Sabbagh, M. & Doody, R. (1994), Laughter and crying in neurological disorders. *Neuropsychiatry, Neuropsychol. & Behav. Neurol.*, 7:243–250.

Sharrett, C. (1996), The horror film in neoconservative culture. In: *The Dread of Difference: Gender and the Horror Film*, ed. B. K. Grant. Austin: University of Texas Press, pp. 253–279.

Sheppard, R. Z. (1975), The japes of wrath: Review of *No Laughing*

Matter: Rationale of the Dirty Joke, 2nd series. Time, Nov. 10, pp. 96–97.

Solnit, A. J. (1987), A psychoanalytic view of play. *The Psychoanalytic Study of the Child*, 42:205–222. New Haven, CT: Yale University Press.

Soulé, M. (1980), Œdipe au cirque devant le numéro de l'Auguste et du Clown blanc. *Rev. Française de la Psychanal.*, 44:99–126.

Spinoza, B. de (1677), *The Collected Works of Spinoza*, ed. E. Curley. Princeton, NJ: Princeton University Press, 1985.

Sroufe, L. A. & Waters, E. (1976), The ontogenesis of smiling and laughter: A perspective on the organization of development in infancy. *Psycholog. Rev.*, 83:173–189.

Sully, J. (1902), *An Essay on Laughter*. London: Longmans/Green.

Sultanoff, S. M. (1994), Choosing to be amusing: Assessing an individual's receptivity to therapeutic humor. *J. Nursing Jocularity*, 4:34–435.

Sutton, D. F. (1994), *The Catharsis of Comedy*. Lanham, MD: Rowman & Littlefield.

Tarachow, S. (1951), Circuses and clowns. *Psychoanalysis and the Social Sciences, Vol. III*, ed. G. Roheim. New York: International Universities Press.

Nathaniel Tarn Papers, Section 2: American Authors. Stanford University Library, Palo Alto, CA.

Theweleit, K., ed. (1987), *Male Fantasies: Volume 1: Women, Floods, Bodies, History* (trans. E. Carter, C. Turner & S. Conway). Minneapolis: University of Minnesota Press.

——— (1989), *Male Fantasies, Volume 2: Male Bodies, Psychoanalyzing the White Terror* (trans. E. Carter, C. Turner & S. Conway). Minneapolis: University of Minnesota Press.

Thompson, B. R. (1990), Appropriate and inappropriate uses of humor in psychotherapy as perceived by certified reality therapists: A Delphi study. *J. Reality Ther.*, 10:59–65.

Thorson, J. & Powell, F. C. (1991), Measurement of sense of humor. *Psycholog. Rep.*, 69:691–702.

Turnbull, C. (1972), *The Mountain People*. New York: Simon & Schuster.

Vargas, M. J. (1961), Uses of humor in group psychotherapy. *Group Psychother.*, 14:198–202.

Ventis, W. L. (1987), Humor and laughter in behavior therapy. In: *Handbook of Humor and Psychotherapy*, ed. W. F. Fry Jr. & W. A. Salameh. Sarasota, FL: Professional Resource Exchange, pp. 149–169.
———with Higbee, G. & Murdock, S. A. (2001), Using humor in systematic desensitization to reduce fear. *J. Gen. Psychol.*, 128:241–256.
Vinocur, J. (1975), Gershon Legman doesn't tell dirty jokes. *Oui*, March:94–96, 126–128.
Weaver, S. T. & Wilson, C. N. (1997), Addiction counselors can benefit from appropriate humor in the work setting. *J. Employment Counsel.*, 34:108–114.
Wertham, F. (1954), *Seduction of the Innocent*. New York: Rinehart.
West, N. (1939), *Day of the Locust*. London: Signet, 1983.
Which humor for doctors? [editorial] (1998), *Lancet*, 9095:1.
Wickberg, D. (1998), *The Senses of Humor: Self and Laughter in Modern America*. Ithaca, NY: Cornell University Press.
Willeford, W. (1969), *The Fool and His Scepter: A Study in Clowns and Jesters and Their Audience*. Evanston, IL: Northwestern University Press.
Williams, W. C. (1949), The best books I read this year: 12 distinguished opinions. *New York Times*, Dec. 4, p. 4BR.
Winnicott, D. W. (1971), *Playing and Reality*. New York: Basic Books.
Zwerling, I. (1955), The favorite joke technique in diagnostic and therapeutic interviewing. *Psychoanal. Quart.*, 24:104–114.

Other Works by Gershon Legman

1941
The language of homosexuality: An American glossary. In: *Sex Variants*, ed. G. W. Henry. New York: Hoeber, 2:1149–1179.

1942
Note on John Stephen Farmer, compiler of *Slang and Its Analogues*. *Notes & Queries*, 182:289.

1943
Note on John S. Farmer. *Notes & Queries*, 3:117–119.

1945

Sex-censorship in the U.S.A.: A letter from America. *Plan: Organ of the British Progressive League* (London), 11:2–9.

1946

Note on Dr. Thomas Bowdler. *Notes & Queries*, 190:215.

1948

The comic books and the public. *Amer. J. Psychother.*, 2/3:437–477.
A word on Caxton's 'Dictes.' The Library, 5th series, 3:155–185.

1949

Institutionalized lynch: The anatomy of the murder-mystery. *Neurotica*, 4:3–20.
Documentation on "Wolf" and "Lobster." *Amer. Speech*, 24:154–156.
Content of a best-seller. *Neurotica*, 5:33–44. Also editorial.
Review of Burton Stevenson's *Home Book of Proverbs. American Speech*, 24,3:210–212.

1950

Epizootics. *Neurotica*, 7:11–18.
"Poontang." *Amer. Speech*, 25:234–235.

1951

The "influencing machine." *Neurotica*, 8:37–38.
The cant of lexicography. *Amer. Speech*, 26:130–137.
'The Horn Book' and other bibliographical problems. *Amer. Aphrodite*, 9:1–18.

1957

The bawdy song—in fact and print. *Explorations*, 7:139–156. Partly reprinted in *Chapbook*, 4:7–16, 24–34.

1958

Curious and Scholarly Books from a Private Library. Sale catalogue. Auribeau.

Anti-Semitica: Curious and Scholarly Books, suppl. Sale catalogue. Valbonne.

1959
"Pills to purge melancholy": A bibliographical note. *Midwest Folklore*, 9:89–102.

1960
Folksongs, fakelore, folkniks, and cash. *Sing Out!* 10(3):29–35.

1965
The Merry Muses of Caledonia. Collected and in part written by Robert Burns, ed. G. Legman. New Hyde Park, NY: University Books.
A summer reading list to end all summer reading lists. *Fact*, 2(4):39–43.

1972
Dokuhotei Nakano: An appreciation. *The Origamian*, 2(2/3/4):2–12.
Secrets of the blintz (folding): Historical and technical. *The Origami Companion*, 4–7: p. 8 in each issue.

1976
Introduction. In: *The Mammoth Cod, and Address to the Stomach Club* by Mark Twain. Milwaukee, WI: Maledicta.
Bawdy monologues and rhymed recitations. *Southern Folklore Quart.*, 40:59–123.
F.A.R.K. (Folklore article reconstruction kit). *J. Amer. Folklore*, 90:199–202.

1979
"First phallus" by E. Petropoulos (trans. G. Legman). *Maledicta*, 3:103–107.
The magic walking stick by V. Randolph & G. Legman. *Maledicta, 3*: 175–176.

1980
Introduction. In: *Children's Humour: A Joke for Every Occasion* by S. McCosh. London: Granada.

1982

A reminiscence. In: *The Art of Mahlon Blaine* by R. Terry. East Lansing, MI: Peregrine.

1988

Trio amoroso. *Libido*, 1:10–14.

1990

Erotic folksongs and ballads: An international bibliography. *J. Amer. Folklore*, 4:245–267.

1999

Fatherly advice. *Libido*, 11(2): 8–9. (Posthumous publication of a letter written by Legman in 1988.)

Unpublished Works

Lapses in Limerick (1935–38).

[pseud.], The Oxford Professor Novels (1939–1940).

[with Tom Painter], Homosexual Prostitution in the United States (1940).

[with John Del Torto], Homosexuality and Toilet Inscriptions: An Analysis (1940–1941)—supplement to Homosexuality and Toilet Inscriptions.

Toward an Historical Bibliography of Sex Technique (1942).

Notes on Masochism (1950).

Unexpurgated Folk-Balladry, British and American: Bibliographical Check-List. Part II: 1800–1961 (1962).

Models of Madness (1967)—supplement to The Fake Revolt.

Unfinished Works

The Ballad: Unexpurgated Folksongs, American and British.

Kryptádia: The Journal of Erotic Folklore.

The Horn Book: Second Series.

The Book of the Machine—A Study of Science Fiction.

Peregrine Penis (autobiography).

Index